SEX
TRAPS

SEX
TRAPS

Dr. Wanda Davis-Turner

Treasure House

An Imprint of
Destiny Image® Publishers, Inc.
P.O. Box 310
Shippensburg, PA 17257-0310

"For where your treasure is,
there will your heart be also." Matthew 6:21

ISBN 1-56043-193-8

For Worldwide Distribution
Printed in the U.S.A.

This book and all other Destiny Image, Revival Press,
and Treasure House books are available
at Christian bookstores and distributors worldwide.

For a U.S. bookstore nearest you, call **1-800-722-6774**.
For more information on foreign distributors,
call **717-532-3040**.

Or reach us on the Internet: **http://www.reapernet.com**

Dedication

I dedicate this book and the ministry thereof to my special "Gammy Babies":

Steven Wayne Davis Fletcher, II
Starr Wendy Fletcher
Jade Wanda Howell
Timothy F. Howell, III

I Love You So Much!

"Gammy"

Acknowledgments

I thank the Lord Jesus for giving me the assignment to "change dirty diapers" in His Kingdom. It is my desire that this book bring glory and honor to Him as men and women, boys and girls, are freed out of their sex traps.

I especially appreciate Andrea Vines, and also Alisha Harrell, who in the ninth hour assisted me with vital reference research.

Special thanks and appreciation to Don and Cathy Nori, Phillip Zook, Keith Carroll, and Larry Walker—my Destiny Image family who believed in this book.

Appreciation

Special thanks to my husband, Bishop Andrew C. Turner, II; and wonderful daughters and sons, Wendy and Steve, Whitney and Timothy, Aniecka and Andrea for your love and support during the past year.

Contents

Introduction

As if guided by the unseen hand of some twisted despot, the American culture has been crafted and molded into one massive trap for the unwary—or as Dr. Wanda Davis-Turner would say—one massive *sex trap*! The "pop psychology" pandered through the media would have us believe that we are powerless to control our hormonal drives, and we have believed it. Now our hormone-driven culture has no place to go but down.

From the womb to the grave, we are targeted to be "used" by others or to become self-centered users and abusers ourselves. It is all done in the name of our newest national god: self-gratification. Many Christians benignly buy the lie and pretend that there is nothing really wrong with the American way of life. "It will pass," we say in our politically correct wisdom. Meanwhile, millions of unborn babies are ruthlessly murdered each year in an attempt to cover guilt and as mute sacrifices to preserve self-centered lifestyles of sexual gratification with few if any boundaries.

Many babies who survive grow up in homes with mothers and fathers who are themselves victims of sex abuse. Some become secret "sexual predators" who subject their seed to unthinkable deeds. This in turn creates a whole new generation of helpless victims who are almost certain to become sexually dysfunctional time bombs, just waiting to explode.

Even the secular world is asking, "What is the cure, and where can we find it?" Dr. Wanda Davis-Turner has earned a reputation for boldly wading into issues that most leaders want to avoid. True to form, the message of *Sex Traps* is unmistakable, confrontational, inspirational, and at times, downright embarrassing. It rings with a divine mandate, an urgent call for a holy people to turn back to God for forgiveness and restoration.

Dr. Davis-Turner dares to go behind the closed doors of our bedrooms, church offices, and secluded motel rooms where so many have convinced themselves that God never sees what they do in darkness. She assures us that Jesus Christ and His Church are God's cure for what ails us, but explains that many in the Church have themselves stumbled into sex traps and are unable to get out on their own. Dr. Davis-Turner sweeps away the camouflage and disguising debris to expose the deadly sex traps awaiting us in our own lives. She shows the trapped how to win their freedom and keep it, and helps the rest of us steer clear of the traps as well.

This book is compelling (after all, it is about sex), refreshing, honest, and ultimately practical. I recommend it to parents, pastors, teenagers, counselors, and youth workers. I especially pray that *Sex Traps* finds its way into the hands of sexual predators and their victims. I know that it will lead both to deliverance, salvation, and healing, and to a new life free of sexual addiction and devilish affliction. I've only met one person who could write a book like this one, and her name is Dr. Wanda Davis-Turner. I thank God for her and for the living Christ who planted this life-changing message in her heart.

Larry H. Walker, Managing Editor
Destiny Image Digest Magazine
Shippensburg, Pennsylvania

Chapter 1

Wake Up, Your Passion Is on Fire!

Somewhere tonight, a gifted and charismatic leader of the Church will stoop from his office of divine service to slide between a stranger's sheets in a secret act of adultery while his wife and children fall into a fitful sleep miles away. Elsewhere in a darkened church office or bishop's quarters, a frightened child will be abused by a revered religious leader trapped in the grips of sexual compulsion and grievous sin. The scars of that secret sin will linger forever in the heart and soul of the innocent victim, while the compulsion of sin drives the fallen spiritual leader on from wicked thought to unthinkable deed.

Thousands of sons and daughters across this land have learned to fear the coming of darkness each night because they know that one or both of their parents may undergo an evil transformation when the sun goes down. They know from painful experience that they may once again become the helpless targets of an adult's relentless and perverted sexual appetite.

Millions have survived the torture of an abusive childhood only to enter a tormented adulthood wracked by shameful memories of sexual abuse, spiritual betrayal, and mental destruction. Many cry out, "When will it stop? How could God allow it?" Yet when someone dares to address the secret sins of deviate and illicit sexual behavior in the *Church*, scores of voices rise in protest and many walk out in disgust. But God says, "When will you open your eyes and accept the truth? Only then can the pain stop—I've already made full provision for your freedom, but first you must accept the truth that I reveal."

Even now as you read these words, there are scores of morally upright men and women of God in the midst of incredible success and unprecedented church growth and ministry, who are being stalked by devilish seducers with a will to corrupt and destroy their marriages and ministries. *You may be one of them.* Will you pass the test of temptation or will you fall into satan's cleverly laid *sex trap*? At this very moment there are thousands of men and women who have already fallen into the devil's ditch of passion. They desperately want to break off their ungodly relationships and resume a righteous walk with God. They long for the strength to be free, but they need help.

Born-again, blood-washed Christians stumble needlessly into sex traps every day. Worst of all, when they fall they will hurt everyone who is close to them or who looks to them for leadership and guidance. Most of them will fall into the pit again and again, seemingly unable to escape satan's grip on their own. Who will help them? Who will dare to tell the truth?

There are also thousands of innocent *victims* longing for a word of hope and searching for a life free of undeserved guilt and shame. Millions of lives, marriages, ministries, and souls are at stake, yet few people seem willing to identify satan's sex traps and warn people away from the snares he has set to ensnare the unwary. I can't hold back any longer. God's message is like a fire burning in my bones, and that is why you are reading these words today.

God apprehended me and forced me to face this issue more than seven years ago while I was resting at a health resort at Ashbury Park in New Jersey. I was taking a walk when the Lord Jesus spoke to my spirit and said, "Wanda, many in My Kingdom have become trapped in sexual sin and misconduct. There is a great need to change people's dirty diapers from pulpit to pew in My Body, and I assign this task to you." I was stunned and amazed, and more than a little confused. As He continued to minister to me, I began to remember the many times hurting men and women in the Body of Christ had come to me for counsel, and for prayer for healing and deliverance. They wanted to bare their souls to someone—to anyone who would listen—concerning the hidden issues, struggles, and sins that involved sex.

Many times after I had conducted conferences or revivals, I would return to my office where a small mountain of letters and phone messages piled up from people who longed to confess and repent of their sins to someone who could help them be set free. It wasn't unusual for me to identify signs of sexual abuse in the sad eyes of little children in this country and abroad. Without exception, something in my spirit would be drawn to them as I reached out in love and prayer.

That divine dialogue in Ashbury Park forever changed my life and the direction of my ministry. When I shared these things with my friend, Dr. Carolyn Harrell, she confirmed through the prophetic word that I would minister to thousands who are afflicted and ensnared by the powers of satan in sex traps. In the two years that followed, this was further confirmed independently by Pastor Sheryl Gilbert of Oakland, California, and Bishop Bernard Jordan of New York City, New York. Perhaps the greatest confirmation came shortly after I left Ashbury Park, on the day I received a telephone call from a precious brother in Christ who was also a noted gospel recording artist and pastor.

I'd never met this pastor before, but somehow he had heard about my ministry and he said that he felt the need to call me. A relationship developed under the orchestration of God that soon led to an invitation to speak at his church in Los Angeles, and at the Gospel Music Workshop held in New Orleans, Louisiana, that year. Some counseled me not to accept the invitations because a number of people in that congregation were reputed to openly live homosexual or lesbian lifestyles. Some warned that I might be committing "ministerial suicide" if I accepted an invitation to be a major speaker at such a church, but God was behind the invitations and I knew it.

First I ministered in the local church with great anointing, and later I flew to New Orleans with a prepared message entitled, "Rest in Stress." But as soon as I'd checked into my room and began to relax, God gave me a new direction. The Spirit of the Lord commanded me to pick up my Bible and notebook, and I heard these words in my heart (my Bible had already opened directly on that text):

> But the wicked are like the tossing sea, which cannot rest, whose waves cast up mire and mud. "There is no peace," says my God, "for the wicked. Shout it aloud, do not hold back. Raise your voice like a trumpet. Declare to My people their rebellion and to the house of Jacob their sins" (Isaiah 57:20–58:1 NIV).

I felt as if I had become God's secretary as He dictated a message entitled, "It's Turning Time." That evening, I entered an auditorium in New Orleans that was packed with thousands of people, and Pastor Kenneth Ulmer of Los Angeles introduced me. What happened next was an experience that I will never forget as long as I live. The moment I stepped behind the podium, I was empowered by the Holy Spirit as never before. "I knew that I knew that I knew" that God had handpicked me for that assignment. I was thrilled as God spoke through me to challenge, confront, comfort, and usher change into the lives of many men and women entangled by sex traps that night. The love of God was almost overpowering as I embraced hundreds of people who came to the altar for prayer and deliverance after I preached, "It's Turning Time."

After I returned to my office in California, I received a flood of letters and phone calls from people who wanted to tell me about their deliverance from lifestyles that were not pleasing to God and that were contrary to His Word. Since then, I have tried to avoid this message at times because of the tremendous cost it requires. Most churches and church leaders aren't ready to hear the truth about sex traps, but there are also multitudes who are either caught in satan's snares, or who are victims of sexual sins. They desperately need to hear the truth and be set free. They need to be told that God is out to meet their need. I have to tell you that this message has brought persecution, misunderstanding, and stress to me and my family, but it has also brought blessed deliverance and healing to thousands. Now it is time for the truth to be told on the printed page.

There are such things as *sex traps*, and like most traps, they are most effective when they are set with the proper *bait* to attract victims. The *bait* that satan uses for sex traps is our own passions! God created our physical bodies and emotional makeup for His own glory and service. Our complex chemical and hormonal systems are easily stimulated or affected by outside factors, and they can ignite incredible fires of passion and motivation in men and women.

Human passions, properly motivated, can birth nations, win wars, defy death, overcome impossible obstacles, and seal a marriage with unbreakable devotion. Improperly directed, they can destroy nations, ignite devastating wars, bring violent death, make even the smallest obstacle impassable, and destroy the best of marriages through callous betrayal, selfishness, and rejection.

God created us to be a passionate people. He wants us to have passionate lifetime love affairs with our spouses. He wants us to passionately follow His footsteps and compassionately heal the sick and restore the fallen. He wants us to preach a passionate gospel backed by unrelenting love and sacrifice for the good of others. As with every other gift of God, satan seeks to twist and distort God's gift of passion, sexual attraction, and the sex act. The devil wants to make your passion a tool of destruction. It is time for all of us to wake up! We must awaken, open our eyes, and discern the time.

Where have you been looking lately? Are your eyes and desires wandering to forbidden fields? Are you clinging to unforgiveness and bitterness toward your spouse and winking at someone else at the office? Are you preaching the gospel on Sunday while gazing at the woman who sits in the second pew—the one who keeps watching you week after week with illicit hunger? Watch out! Your passions are on fire with a strange fire, and you are about to fall into satan's *sex trap*!

The satanic entanglements of sex traps can affect every area of our lives. Although Christians aren't very comfortable when the topic of sex comes up, most of them are interested anyway. They need to be, because the road they walk each day is littered with dangerous snares, detours, blind alleys, and seductive enticements engineered to accomplish one thing: to trap and ensnare God's beloved.

The social structure of the United States, the European nations, and much of the Caribbean is riddled with the hellish idea that "if it feels good, do it." This idea permeates our television programs, talk shows, newspapers, and magazines. It dominates the thinking of our teenagers as well as of most adults. Almost every kind of sexual liaison is winked at today, but several decades ago it would have been called what it is: sin. Thinking people, visionary people, godly people know that sin destroys everything it touches. Runaway sin is threatening to destroy our homes, our marriages, our churches, and society itself. I have good news for you: There is a sure cure for the sexual sin that is eating away at our lives and future, but it will hurt. It will cost you and I something to be free, but Jesus gave us a clear diagnosis of our problem and a wonderful promise of a cure: "The thief cometh not, but for to steal, and to kill, and to destroy: I am come that they might have life, and that they might have it more abundantly" (Jn. 10:10).

There is a thief who is out to steal everything that is dear to you and to your heavenly Father, but he is powerless as long as you and I walk in obedience to God. Unfortunately, too many of us are like the Israelites of old who had been given a promised land but who couldn't resist reaching beyond the fence to grasp for the forbidden fruit that offends God:

Ye shall make you no idols nor graven image, neither rear you up a standing image, neither shall ye set up any image of stone in your land, to bow down unto it: for I am the

Lord your God. ... But if ye will not hearken unto Me, and will not do all these commandments; and if ye shall despise My statutes, or if your soul abhor My judgments, so that ye will not do all My commandments, but that ye break My covenant: I also will do this unto you; I will even appoint over you terror, consumption, and the burning ague, that shall consume the eyes, and cause sorrow of heart: and ye shall sow your seed in vain, for your enemies shall eat it (Leviticus 26:1,14-16).

Four thousand years ago, God led His chosen people out of bondage because of His great love for them. True to His nature, He wanted only good for them. He wanted them to possess all the liberty and joy He had to offer (which is more than we can even imagine or absorb). Yet the Israelites insisted on clinging to deaf and dumb idols made of stone and wood.

Today, we are faced with the same basic situation in the Church. Jesus sacrificed Himself to provide the *abundant life,* but many of us insist on clinging to our sordid affairs that wring the life out of our spouses and innocent children. We run to the VCR to watch sexually explicit films and then fantasize about another person's spouse. We misuse and abuse our authority to dominate others, or we are one of the many victims of such abuse. It is *turning time,* beloved. God has done His part; now He is turning the spotlight on us with full force. No longer will our secret sins remain secret— He is exposing our sin and demanding an answer. He is forcing us to make a choice because He has a greater agenda and plan for this earth. He wants you and me to play our part in it, but while He forgives sin, He will not tolerate sin.

I have received a divine commission to expose the sex traps that I see and to snatch prisoners out of their sex traps in Jesus' name, and I am anointed by the Holy Ghost to proclaim healing to the wounded victims and children of those caught up in sex traps. The next order of business is to find out where you stand today. Are you ready to examine yourself? If you want the abundant life, if you want to walk with God and never look back, then it is time to examine your life today. It is never too late. No sin is too great for Jesus to forgive and wash away, but God will not tolerate halfhearted commitment or falsehood. If you are serious, then turn to the next chapter and examine your heart for signs that lead to sexual addiction and sex traps.

Chapter 2

Five Roads That Lead to Sex Traps

Sex is big.

Just ask the advertising folks on Madison Avenue in New York City. Sex has been at the top of their "best-seller" list since advertising was invented. Advertisers have used sex to sell everything from automobiles and cigarettes to presidential candidates, fluoride toothpaste, and time-share condominiums.

Let's look at the word *sex*. I asked the Lord, "What is sex?" I know I should know the answer already, but I wanted to make sure that I wasn't missing anything. The answer was, "It is the thing that is trapping so many believers today because sex is the intimate exchange of physical, emotional, and spiritual parts or properties with or without consent."

Sex embodies all of those ideas associated with sexual relationships. Many words and phrases come to mind when we think of sex: sexual attraction, sex appeal, magnetism, sensuality, affinity, love, courtship, marriage, and reproduction (just to name a few). Sexuality, masculinity, femininity, womanliness, manhood, and manliness also come to mind when we think of the word *sex*. I've gathered together a number of important statements made about the subject of sex by two Christian leaders and authors whom I respect.

Many of us in the Body of Christ are uncomfortable with discussions about sex, but Dr. Edwin Louis Cole says, "In our society, sex is a subject that is pretty hard to avoid! From infancy, a child's perception of sex is shaped by videos, music, magazines, billboards, films, television, peers, and school curriculums. Most of these named above depict sex as something other than God's original plan for sex."[1]

"God's plan for sex was of course for procreation which is the method in which a relationship between husband and wife would be utilized to expand God's image in history....Children are not given to us so that only we can be duplicated, but more important children are given us in marriage so that God's image can be transferred on earth. Parents are to stamp the image of God on their children so that when those children leave home, God's image and presence has been expanded in history....By now, you must realize that sex is God's idea and therefore it is good!"[2]

"Sex is a legitimate passion given to us by God."[3]

"In fact, sex is part of your God-given makeup, but it was never intended to be your master."[4]

"When sex becomes our master, it results in tremendous human suffering, death, and expense to society."[5]

"Broken homes, dysfunctional families and an entire generation seeking drugs, gangs, and sexual promiscuity in place of love and intimacy are some of the results."[6]

"Satan has literally taken this God-given gift and sought to pervert it, counterfeit it and imitate it as only he can do. So men lose their virginity trying to validate their manhood. Women sacrifice their purity seeking for someone to love and accept them. We have bought Satan's lie that immediate sexual gratification, regardless of the long-term cost, ought to be the driving force in our lives. The price tag for this purchase is high...high in medical costs for AIDS and sexually transmitted diseases (STDs)."[7]

In fact, according to research done by the A.C. Green Foundation for Youth and the Center for Disease Control and other agencies, approximately 50 different sexually transmitted diseases are continuing to spread like wildfire.[8] They report that one of them, syphilis, has been 100 percent curable for years, yet today it is at an all-time high, raging with greater fury than ever before. Why? Because of sex traps! They say that one in four Americans will contract a sexually transmitted disease, and that two-thirds of those diseases will occur in people under the age of 25.[9]

"Every day it is estimated that over 15,000 high school students in America are infected with at least one of these STD diseases. HPV [human papilloma virus], which causes cervical and penis cancer, was found in 46 percent of young women who attended the University of California, Berkeley. Every person involved in an extramarital or premarital affair runs a 50 percent risk of catching a disease, not to mention the chances of an unwanted pregnancy, which numbers over a million each year."[10]

I know that there is a good chance you may think that condoms are the answer. After all, our government has thrown millions of dollars into the effort to convince us that a lie is truth. Dr. Edwin Louis Cole relied on scientific research data when he wrote, "Condoms cannot stop sexually transmitted diseases that spread from outside contact such as syphilis, herpes, and crabs, to name a few."[11] "The HIV virus itself is 450 times smaller than a sperm cell, about one-fifth the size of the holes in latex—the material from which the best condoms are made. Condoms also fail up to 36% of the time against pregnancies for those depending on them the most...young people!"[12]

The high price of sex traps continues to climb higher as they send people to professional counselors, and as they send unwanted unborn children to abortionists. They raise the welfare cost because the government must pay to take care of children who don't have a pair of parents to watch over them. *Sex traps* raise the cost even higher by increasing the divorce rate after the pain of deceit, infidelity, and broken covenants becomes too great for men and women in marriage.[13] Whenever we as created people take what the Creator has given for our "good" and pervert it, we, in a sense, have devastated and destroyed God's original plans to bless us.

And yet, with all the data I've mentioned, why would an advertising copywriter try so hard to work sex into an advertisement for motor oil or engine parts? There is only one reason: He believes that sex will capture the reader's interest and draw attention to his client's product. What does sex have to do with valve rings or motor oil? Check out the automotive magazines at your local grocery or convenience store. How many bikini-clad ladies have you seen changing the oil or doing a valve job on their cars in your neighborhood?

It's called sex appeal. Some folks try to disguise it by removing the magical three-letter word and calling it "physical and emotional attraction" (but everyone knows they're *really* talking about sex). Whatever you want to call it, it was put there by God. Sexual attraction and desire is normal. Let me say that again for some of my more religious readers: Sexual attraction and desire is normal.

Sex is a good thing, not an evil thing. It is a God-given gift, not a devil-spawned curse. I think that the Church was pulled crosswise on this issue because people discovered sometime early in Adam and Eve's lifetime that sexual desire is a continual thing—it doesn't really have an "off" button. Once the switch turns on around the age of 12 or 13 (or earlier), you have to be careful who you get close to and under what circumstances.

God was the Master Chemist who cooked up the hormone idea and installed it in our race—not the devil. (Satan could not be trusted with his own chemistry set; besides, all he knows how to do is tinker with what God has already made.) The same God who created Adam and Eve also fitted them with their respective reproductive systems and sex drives. If you haven't noticed, He put them *together* when He lit the fuse to the firecracker. He saw them as *one flesh*, even though two distinct individuals were involved. God put a strong attraction and desire in men and women so they would perpetuate the race and confront life's challenges outside the garden *together*.

One problem is that some of us don't know whether to thank God for the blessing of sex or petition Him for deliverance from its curse. (I know which one I vote for.) Most of this confusion is rooted in outright ignorance of God's plan for sex and sexual desire. Another problem is our indiscriminate release of sexual signals (or "open for business" signs in some cases) in inappropriate ways and places.

There is a definite problem present even in the Body of Christ. It is the world's unceasing pressure on us (women especially) through the media and advertising to look alluring, sexy, and attractive to the opposite sex. The spirit behind this pressure pushes precious women of God who minister through music or the Word to distract men through their attire right in the middle of a worship service.

I can't tell you how many times I have fumed my way through a long worship service in conferences around the country while sitting beside my husband, Bishop Andrew Turner. No, I wasn't being unspiritual. I was infuriated with what was being waved in front of my face—and my husband's. Have you ever been forced to watch the barely covered, wildly wiggling backsides of enthusiastic women leading worship on stage? The problem wasn't that they were women, or that they were enthusiastic. The problem is that we have not all been taught how to dress, move, and behave as Christian men and women in a public service.

Often, I think that many of us are not even aware of what we are really doing. We don't know that our "tight dress, dips and splits, bra-less look" suggests and invites sexual attention. I have often wanted to interrupt the service so I could "prophesy" to the misled: "Ladies, we are here to offer a sacrifice of praise to the Lord—not a sacrifice of flesh to the lustful. Rein it in!" Now brothers, you are not exempt either. Many of you deliberately "dress to trap" also.

I've challenged women in meetings and conferences across America by speaking to them in their own language of no-nonsense terms:

> "Ladies, can I talk to you for a minute? When you are praise singers in the church or the temple, you need to put a girdle on your fine, wonderfully created self. You are bringing the sacrifice of praise into the house of the Lord. Now what are you doing in the face of the man and the woman of God? I don't care if you are a size 4, size 6, size 16, or size 20. Put something

on it! You can't wear just anything you please and do everything you want to do on stage just because you like it. Direct the attention of every man and woman in the house back to the God of the house, not to your backside or front side, or your dress size. If you want those eyes on you, then you need to get yourself off that stage! If you want those eyes on Jesus, then wrap up those distractions."

Our loose tongues and wandering eyes are another problem in the Church. When I say loose tongues, I'm not talking about gossip or slander (that is another book at least); I am talking about foolish revelations of very private and holy things. As fine as my husband is, and he is very fine, I am not going to tell you or any other person the details of just how fine he is in the home or bedroom. That is private, sacred, and exclusive to my husband and myself. I shudder when I hear a woman spilling the private details of her marriage relationship to a room full of women at a beauty shop or church function. It only baits another sex trap of the imagination for the unwary and unwise.

Wandering eyes have wreaked havoc in God's house for centuries. King David got in trouble with wandering eyes, so what makes us think that we can get away with it? I am convinced that I am married to the finest man on the earth, but that doesn't mean I don't notice when another fine man walks into a place. I have eyes, and I know another fine man when I see one. The key is that I know which fine man is mine, and which one isn't. I know that "one ain't mine," so I don't keep looking.

A lot of Christians fall into traps because they deceive themselves with false statements and beliefs. They think that when they get saved and filled with the Holy Ghost that they become immune to all temptation. I wish it was so, but it isn't. The truth is that we are human. We need to obey God's Word and keep watch on our flesh and our eyes.

For all that is in the world, the lust of the flesh, and the lust of the eyes, and the pride of life, is not of the Father, but is of the world. And the world passeth away, and the lust thereof: but he that doeth the will of God abideth for ever (1 John 2:16-17).

God put sexual desire in the human race so we would have the ability to share and give intimately to one another. Desire in and of itself is not evil; it is normal. There are two errors that have caused incredible damage in the Church over the last few centuries. The first is the idea that sex is dirty and unclean. The second is the thought that *real* Christians aren't affected by sexual desire. The line goes, "Just pray, read the Bible, and go to church—and the opposite sex won't appeal to you." That's a lie.

Sexual desire is not evil until it becomes twisted into a lustful obsession for sheer physical gratification. The key to whether desire is good or bad depends on the direction it takes. When sexual desire is channeled in the right direction (God's direction), then that desire, or "urge to merge," can lead to the establishment of a happy Christian home where God's command that we "multiply and replenish the earth" is joyfully obeyed. God-given sexual desire in men and women is the motivating factor behind the verse in the Book of Genesis that says, "Therefore shall a man leave his father and his mother, and shall cleave unto his wife: and they shall be one flesh" (Gen. 2:24). Desire channeled in this direction pleases God and results in a man-woman relationship that is healthy and filled with love and mutual respect.

Tragedy results when our desires take us away from God's original plan for sexual union and communion within the bonds of the marriage covenant. Desire fulfilled outside of marriage creates crippling shame, alienation from loved ones, blame-shifting, and even the tendency to arrogantly manipulate others for personal pleasure. In my experience, people caught in a sex trap will have a pronounced lack of self-control in their lives. They quickly become *addicts* who devote or surrender themselves to their sin habitually or obsessively.[14] They seem unable to say "no" to their selfish desires. They have fallen under the influence of sin, and there are five broad roads leading to most sex traps.

The Five Roads That Lead to Sex Traps

In my years of counseling and praying with people caught in sex traps, nearly all of them admit that they didn't *plan* to sin, but they started on a course that ultimately landed them in a trap. In most cases, one of the five things listed below led them away from God's way to the path of sin.

Number 1: A fascination with and compulsive desire for the forbidden.

This motivation goes all the way back to the garden of Eden when the snake tempted Eve with the *one forbidden thing* in all of paradise. Eve ignored the bliss of paradise in her fascination with the forbidden. Once she possessed the forbidden, she lost God's greatest blessing. You would think that we would have learned something from her mistake.

Number 2: A compulsive need for ego fulfillment—even if the thing that fulfills is illegal or illicit.

The man who keeps going to a prostitute knows that woman doesn't really like him. He knows that she is just putting on an act to get his money, but he doesn't care. He wants to be noticed and feel needed. He wants to feel like a real man for a few minutes, and the prostitute flatters his ego by making him think that he is somebody special. All along of course, it is just another sex trap. One more human has been seduced by the enemy of his soul into seeking ego fulfillment in the arms of sin.

Illegal ego fulfillment can take place long before sexual addiction enters the picture. You may have a seemingly wonderful relationship with God and not even be aware that you have a problem. How many average women have become addicted to the trap of being "noticed by men" so that they will feel like real women? They always dress to impress and to win compliments and flattery from men. At the height of their compulsion, they may even find themselves walking slow and slinky toward the church door to greet the pastor and secretly hoping that his wife isn't there. Their eyes drip with illicit promises and unspoken availability as they say, "Pastor, it is *so good* to see you—it has been a very hard week for me." Then the pastor unknowingly provides the response they want to hear, "Well, Sister Brown, you sure don't show it, praise the Lord. You look lovely this morning." On a bad day when the pastor's guard is down and his wife is out of town, he may agree to help when the slinky woman says, "Pastor, I would feel *so much better* if you would pray for me at my home today..."

Number 3: The world's unceasing pressure on us (women especially) through the media and advertising to look alluring, sexy, and attractive to the opposite sex.

We are in serious trouble if our personal identity is linked directly to our success in generating sexual appeal. Yet that is exactly what the media portray as "the way it is." Women everywhere—in the church foyer and on the street corner—compete with each other to look fashionable and to do everything they can to attract stares of men. This shameful practice runs rampant in our churches, and it is shocking to see what this unclean spirit causes our beautiful young Christian girls to wear.

We have allowed the skewed morals of the world to taint God's house, our homes, and our thinking. Women will dress provocatively to excite the fantasies of men in the church by entering God's house in scanty outfits designed to get their attention. To be specific, I have seen women prancing down the aisles with everything "hanging out." I've seen them come in with no bras, no panties, no girdles, no jockey shirts, and no T-shirts. There is no excuse for it. Illicit sex and sexual attention from the opposite sex never has and never will fulfill a person's need. Fulfillment and true self-worth only comes when you accept yourself as God accepts you. You will never be who you really can be until you acknowledge who God says you are. (Men can be just as bad with their tight jeans or dress slacks, and with their openly lustful glances—or stares—at every female in God's house.)

Number 4: The lie that says, "You deserve to have some fun. Reward yourself."

The devil is quick to tell you that you deserve some fun—if he is sure that it will lead to sin. Solomon did some astounding things with the wisdom that he received from God. David brought Israel into power, but Solomon brought her into prominence. He not only built the nation to unequaled economic greatness, but King Solomon also constructed the temple of God. Unfortunately, as he looked around at all of his great accomplishments, satan slipped in with his time-proven lie and used Solomon's pride to bypass his wisdom.

The world's wisest man began to tell himself, "I deserve a reward." His first mistake was to take credit for God's accomplishment, and his second was that he began lusting after the very women whom God had forbidden the Israelites to marry because they came from idolatrous nations. In his pride, Solomon assumed that, because he was king, he could ignore God's law. His "reward" was to break God's law and join himself body and soul with devil-worshiping women. It cost him his kingdom and doomed Israel to destruction. Even the world's wisest man tried to justify his sin by telling himself that he deserved it. It didn't work for him either, because he was in a sex trap!

Number 5: The flesh's continual craving for "variety."

Again, you and I can learn from Solomon's colossal mistakes. Even a quick examination of his life story in the Scriptures should tell us that *variety is not the spice of life.* Sexual addiction is like any other addiction—the more you get the more you want (and the less capacity you have to ever be satisfied). That is because the secret of "great sex" has more to do with a great relationship based on mutual love and respect in an *exclusive* lifelong commitment than on the mechanical parts and motions involved.

The desire for "variety" will drive people to obsessive behavior because once addicted to variety, they have lost their capacity to be satisfied. King Solomon is the perfect example of a man destroyed by the quest for "variety" in the sexual realm.

> *But king Solomon loved many strange women, together with the daughter of Pharaoh, women of the Moabites, Ammonites, Edomites, Zidonians, and Hittites; of the nations concerning which the Lord said unto the children of Israel, Ye shall not go in to them, neither shall they come in unto*

you: for surely they will turn away your heart after their gods: Solomon clave unto these in love. And he had seven hundred wives, princesses, and three hundred concubines: and his wives turned away his heart. For it came to pass, when Solomon was old, that his wives turned away his heart after other gods: and his heart was not perfect with the Lord his God, as was the heart of David his father (1 Kings 11:1-4).

Solomon couldn't handle it and neither can you. Sister, if you mess with one or a dozen ungodly men, they will turn your heart away from God. Brother, it you mess with one or a harem of ungodly women, they will turn your heart away from God. God's plan is so simple and pure that we like to overlook it or "rewrite" it to suit our wishes. He ordained that one man and one woman unite for life. Period. If you do things God's way, you will get all the "variety" you can handle.

Let me set something straight: Many Christians think that God does not want you sleeping around with everybody because sex is not fun. What planet did they come from? *Sex is good, and sex is fun.* It is a wonderful "sit-u-a-tion." (Now I know you're saved, but you are not *that* saved!) Since I've gathered some momentum, I might as well indulge in a little shock therapy. I have to share a truth with you: Did you know that the Lord allows orgasms in the married couples of the Body of Christ? Yes, your moments of sexual intimacy in marriage should be interludes of ecstasy and not "duty nights." In fact, married women in the Body of Christ should be frequent shoppers at Victoria's Secret stores to prepare to "function at the junction" with their husbands.

One of the reasons that you and I should not be promiscuous sexually is that in God's eyes (and in ancient Jewish custom), the true marriage ceremony takes place on the first night of sexual intimacy. In ancient biblical times, couples did not have large wedding parties with flower girls and ring bearers. Neither did they go into debt spending money that they didn't have trying to impress people whom they didn't know with large, expensive weddings. Actually, the wedding ceremony was the physical act of sexual intimacy when the groom became joined to his bride as they "functioned at the junction." Now, if sex joins a man to a woman, and a woman to a man...*then every time you have sex, there is a type of joining, a type of marriage.* There must be a lot of bigamists in God's house who desperately need to be freed from their sex trap of promiscuity, fornication, and adultery.

Endnotes

1. Edwin Louis Cole, *The Glory of Sex* (Tulsa, Oklahoma: Honor Books, 1993), p. 11.

2. Cole, *The Glory of Sex*, p. 9.

3. Cole, *The Glory of Sex*, p. 18.

4. Cole, *The Glory of Sex*, p. 8.

5. Tony Evans, *Tony Evans Speaks Out on Sexual Purity* (Chicago: Moody Press, 1995), p. 18.

6. Cole, *The Glory of Sex*, p. 11.

7. Evans, *Tony Evans Speaks Out*, p. 7.

8. Cole, *The Glory of Sex*, quoting statistics provided in A.C. Green's foreword to this book, p. 12.

9. Cole, *The Glory of Sex*, drawn from statistics quoted on p. 12.

10. Cole, *The Glory of Sex*, p. 12.

11. Cole, *The Glory of Sex*, p. 12.

12. Cole, *The Glory of Sex*, p. 13.

13. From ideas presented by Evans in *Tony Evans Speaks Out*, p. 7.

14. *Merriam Webster's Collegiate Dictionary*, 10th ed. (Springfield, Massachusetts: Merriam-Webster, Inc., 1994), p. 13.

Chapter 3

Traps, Trappers, and Trappees

Blessed be the Lord, who hath not given us as a prey to their teeth. Our soul is escaped as a bird out of the snare of the fowlers: the snare is broken, and we are escaped. Our help is in the name of the Lord, who made heaven and earth (Psalm 124:6-8).

This passage speaks prophetically to each of us about four powerful truths.

1. **The Lord "...hath not given us as a prey..."** (Ps. 124:6).

God said that we don't belong in the devil's jaws—or in anybody else's, for that matter. The Hebrew word for "prey" here is *tereph*. It literally means "something torn, a fragment, a fresh leaf, prey, food."[1] In the context of *sex traps*, you might as well think of it as "fresh meat." God is saying that He never intended for us to be "fresh meat" for the devil or any sexual predator in the world or in the Church. If you haven't figured it out yet, the subject of sex traps is deadly serious.

2. **"Our soul is escaped as a bird out of the snare..."** (Ps. 124:7).

Praise God for providing an escape for each of us. First Corinthians 10:13 declares, "There hath no temptation taken you but such as is common to man: but God is faithful, who will not suffer you to be tempted above that ye are able; but will with the temptation also make a way to escape, that ye may be able to bear it."

Our "way out" is so simple that we very often miss it. Paul simply advises us to "flee fornication" (1 Cor. 6:18a). In other words, "Run, baby, run!" Move up, out, and away. Change your address, get a new telephone number, relocate to a new city if necessary. But whatever you do, remove yourself from the person, the environment, and the temptation that seeks to destroy you and your relationship with God.

Constantly seek to remind yourself that you are "bought with a price: therefore glorify God in your body, and in your spirit, which are God's" (1 Cor. 6:20).

3. "The snare [trap] is broken..." (Ps. 124:7).

This verse prophetically declares that satan's trap is broken because God's power is greater than the jaws or teeth of any demonic trap. The power of Jesus literally breaks the snares set for us. Don't believe satan's lie, "I've got you and I won't let you go." God has already set you free—get up and run. When you can't remove the trap—remove *yourself* from the trap.

4. "...We are escaped. Our help is in the name of the Lord..." (Ps. 124:7-8).

"Just a minute—I'm a little confused. If I've escaped from my snare and the Lord has broken the snare (the trap), then why do I still need help?" It is because the Lord only set our soul free. Now you and I face the task of freeing our bodies too.

Dr. Tony Evans shares that the body and spirit are closely linked. For the Christian, sex is a spiritual issue. You cannot worship God on Sunday and enter sexual immorality on Monday. You can't keep those separate, because your body—not just your spirit—is for the Lord. So now we also face the task of gathering up and destroying the broken pieces of the snares and traps in our life. If we don't, then satan, the enemy of our soul, may repair the pieces of our broken traps, freshen the bait, and catch us again!

Many of us have been set free, but we continue to hang around the broken traps that still have the bait that our carnal minds, emotions, and flesh crave. My mother used to tell me in my teenage years, "Wanda, always get home before midnight." When I was grown but not yet married, she used to say, "Wanda, always get home before two o'clock, 'cause honey, after two o'clock, ain't nothing open but legs." That's pretty raw, but she was warning me about a trap of the devil. You are open prey for the snare of the devil when you refuse to heed good wisdom and advice.

The problem is that a lot of Christians don't know the danger that they are in. And they have no idea that God has already made a way of escape. Christians are being trapped in sex traps by the thousands, and many have even become trappers themselves. This doesn't line up with God's Word. God says that He has broken the snares set against us, and that we have escaped to freedom. We know that God doesn't lie or make mistakes, so we have to point our accusing fingers back toward ourselves. Something is seriously wrong.

There are countless numbers of snares and traps out there, and we need to learn what they are and how they work. Then we need to remember that our help is in the Lord. I am not a hunter or woods person, but I know how to ask questions and do research. There are at least four major types of snares and traps. (If you are an expert, please forgive my very general treatment of this subject—I am sure that there are many more, but every new type you could point out to me would only strengthen my point and highlight the seriousness of our situation.)

Now, what is a trap? It is an apparatus or scheme designed to catch, to ensnare, to hold, and to possess for the supreme purpose of destroying its victim. Some traps are right out in the open, but most are hidden from sight in hopes that the victim will come to the wrong place at the wrong time. Every snare and trap in existence relies on familiarity and false assumptions to succeed. One assumption that the devil can almost always count on with Christians goes something like this: "Oh, *that* will never happen to me, because I would *never* do that kind of thing. I know others fell for it, but I'm *different*."

Four Major Types of Snares and Traps

1. *Snare*—"A kind of trap for small animals, usually consisting of a noose which jerks tight upon the release of a spring trigger; anything dangerous, risky, etc. that tempts or attracts; a thing by which a person is entangled; a trap."[2] Larger versions of snares use camouflaged nets attached to a large bent sapling. When the trigger is activated, the tree is released and the nets swoop up the prey and suspend it above the ground in the closed net until capture.

2. *Box trap*—This trap uses a suspended box held up by a stick attached to a baited trigger. When the bait is taken or the trigger disturbed, the box suddenly falls on the prey, trapping it inside.

3. *Pit trap*—A pit trap is used for larger and more dangerous prey. It is almost always placed along a regularly traveled path. A deep pit is dug with steep sides, and is then covered with a flimsy structure and hidden with leaves or light branches that look "normal" but are unable to hold the weight of the prey. These traps are made even more effective when bait is placed suspended over the hidden pit or on the opposite side from where the prey is expected to travel.

4. *Box canyon, boxed-enclosure trap*—Hunters often use box canyons that have no exit on one end, or a fenced or walled area funneling down to a closed end to capture large numbers of prey, or to capture very mobile or quick prey. These traps often use the naturally occurring terrain of the prey's environment to either entrap the prey or to kill the prey by ambush.

All traps and snares rely either on bait to attract prey, or on the existing traffic along well-traveled paths. Most of the time, trappers choose paths that lead to vital resources such as water sources and feeding grounds; or to strong "likes" such as high ground, salt licks, or mating areas. The assumption is that the attention of the prey is so focused on the satisfaction of a need or want that unusual circumstances or devices are ignored and assumed harmless.

If all this information about bait, traps, and prey makes you uncomfortable, then I've accomplished my goal. It is ironic that one of the best descriptions of a sex trap comes to us through Solomon, a man who fell harder than anyone into—you guessed it—a *sex trap*.

The seventh chapter of Proverbs best illustrates this sex trap. Solomon allows us to observe the actions of a young man described as "simple" and "void of understanding" who falls headlong into satan's snare. He slips through the streets and into the private bedroom of a harlot. Loud and stubborn, the harlot catches the man, kisses him, and entices him to spend a night of passion, lust, and sensuality that led to "...hell, going down to the chambers of death" (Prov. 7:27).

Sexual trappers and trappees come in many forms, and most have the potential to become sexual predators because of their constantly growing hunger and addiction. They include those compulsively addicted to pornographic movies and "adult" books; child molesters, exhibitionists, indecent phone callers, voyeurs or "Peeping Toms," nymphomaniacs, and "Johns," the customers habitually driven to seek out prostitutes.

All of these people are both the victims of traps and the trappers themselves, and they often lead double and triple lives filled with crippling guilt and hopelessness. Where does it end? It can all end with *knowledge*—knowledge about who you are and who God is; knowledge about what God says about you.

God says you were "fearfully and wonderfully made" (Ps. 139:14). I don't care if you have a wide nose, thin nose, fat nose, flat nose, or beautiful nose. I don't care if you are black, yellow, white, or brown. You may be thin, fat, short, or tall. You need to tell yourself and the devil, "Listen, I am fearfully and wonderfully made. I am somebody special. I am created in the image of God. I am not a biological mistake or an untimely accident. I'm here on earth with purpose, promise, and destiny." You may be a wounded victim or a compulsive trapper who preys on the unsuspecting innocent—but you can be free today if you repent and turn to God. The Lord says in the Bible that He knew you before you were formed in your mother's womb (see Jer. 1:5). He knows the number of hairs on your head, and He gave you fingerprints and a dental composition that no one else in the universe has ever had. You are wonderful, unique, and special. Jesus died to set you free, and that freedom is only a life-changing choice away.

As beautiful as you are, I caution you to remember that God has rules that govern how we use what we have been given. Let's look at some prominent sex traps.

For by means of a whorish woman a man is brought to a piece of bread: and the adulteress will hunt for the precious life. Can a man take fire in his bosom, and his clothes not be burned? Can one go upon hot coals, and his feet not be burned? (Proverbs 6:26-28).

"The adulteress will hunt for the precious life." When the spirit of adultery gets on you, you will go from one sexual experience to another. You will forfeit the beauty, satisfaction, and protection that God provides in marital intimacy. I was leaving a regional ministerial meeting at a city civic center one time when a detective from that city's police department came up to me and said, "Reverend Wanda, I need to talk to you. You need to understand that there is a message that the Church is not getting out. Ministers just have to start teaching and preaching it. This might be uncomfortable for you to hear, but I've got to tell you."

I said, "What is this message?" He said, "You all need to start talking about sex and what it does to people in and out of the church." I told him, "Sir, this preacher is already doing it. But why do you have a special interest?" Then he told me about a case that his department had just dealt with, which I will pass along to you.

There was a beautiful single black woman in Los Angeles, who was well on her way up the ladder of success. She came to a stoplight on Slauson near Crenshaw in her new BMW, and noticed three fine-looking black businessmen in the car next to her. These beautiful black brothers (I call them hometown heroes) were all dressed in business suits, but they weren't too stuffy to nod and flirt with the woman. They said, "Do you want to take a drive with us?"

The woman said, "Yes, I'll come," and she followed them in her car to their condominium on the beach. She consented to have sex with one of the men, but not all three. (This may be shocking to you, but the longer our society tries to function and define right and wrong apart from God, the worse it will get. These people were acting out the "right is what pleases me" philosophy that has swept through this country in the last three decades.) The other two men were doing some "middle-class drugs" because they were men on the rise and they figured that since they had the money, they could do it. They forgot, or didn't care, that chemicals diminish your ability to think and set up boundaries for your life. When you put chemicals in your system, you are bypassing God's built-in protection system and you will do things that you never dreamed you would do. So the two men who were "left out" were high, and they were watching this woman do her thing with their friend. They decided to get in on it—whether the woman agreed or not. The men forced her to have vaginal, anal, and oral sex with them until they were satisfied.

The woman left their place and immediately went to the police to file a rape report on the two men. When the police asked her how many men were present, she said, "There were three men, but I only consented to have sex with one of them. I didn't consent to sexual relations with his two friends." California law requires that anyone who reports that she (or he) has been raped must be checked for infection with sexually transmitted diseases (STDs).

The black police officer looked at me with sadness at this point in the story and said, "Here are three black businessmen. Some mama prayed and worked, and sacrificed so they could go to college, but now it's all wasted. For in a moment of lustful pleasure when those men used that woman to satisfy their sexual urges, they now share the syphilis, gonorrhea, chlamydia trachomitis, and HIV infections that she had before she met them. They slept with the woman; now they will die with her."

Brothers and sisters in Christ—when you sleep with someone, you are also sleeping with everyone else whom that person has already slept with. You may respond, "Well, that doesn't affect us in the Church. We are covered with the blood." Although I believe in the power of the blood, I also believe that *God says what He means.* You can get baptized in water and be filled with the Holy Spirit. You can sing in the choir or preach at every church service you attend. You can woo and win a beautiful wife or husband in the church and still see your spouse die from one of the diseases you picked up from someone in your past because of one wrong choice or decision.

That officer broke down and told me, "Reverend Wanda, you must tell them that they have to stop. There is no 'safe sex.' There is only protective sex in God in a marriage. God said, 'Marriage is honourable in all, and the bed undefiled' (Heb. 13:4a). That is the only place it is not defiled." Any sexual activity outside of the marriage covenant is fornication, adultery, or perversion. It defiles the spirit as well as the body because it *joins* the individuals involved in a spiritual tie. Those young men in California were consumed because they chose to do what they wanted to do instead of what they ought to do.

Pornography is another deadly sex trap. Many a preacher has retired to a hotel room after a powerful meeting where the glory of God fell. Thinking that they would watch some TV before drifting off to sleep, they flip to the Playboy Channel or to some of those "Late Night Spice" adult cable channels. If they linger even 20 seconds, the urge will be on them all night, and every night after that, to "just check out what outrageous things they're doing now." The justification is, "Well, I gotta watch it so I can know what I'm preachin' against." No, you don't, Preacher. You need to guard and protect your spirit as well as your mind. If you don't, then you too may end up in a sex trap, needing to be delivered. You know all you need to know, and now you're messing with what you shouldn't know!

The Internet has turned into a whole new SinNet too. Just like the television, the magazine, and the telephone, the Internet can be used for incredible evil. It contains the most explicit and uncensored sexual depravity ever known. It lays a private communication line for illicit activities right into the privacy of your home or office. Yet it also contains the gospel of Jesus Christ and most of the recorded knowledge of the human race. As with every other medium of mass communication, the moral level of the Internet varies directly with the morals of the end-user.

A sex trap uses a spiritual noose baited with physical enticements. The Lord told me that our bondage starts with the first lingering look. "You have wondered how people in My Kingdom have been trapped. It starts in a hotel room watching a so-called 'adult movie' or lingering over pornography in a public restroom. It begins in a backseat after dark or in a bar in a distant town. It has a spirit in it, and if you look at it or toy with it long enough, that spirit will transfer onto you! Before you know it, you will seek it out everywhere you go. If you can't find it, you will go buy it or take it with you to satisfy your burning lust." We see this all too often as so-called "circuit ministers" travel with their private harems from coast to coast and conference to conference.

That ability to "transfer" to an open soul is why you should never "sit" under the ministry of someone you know is consistently committing adultery, or practicing a homosexual lifestyle. I guarantee you that God can and does deliver His children from homosexuality, but why should you go through that painful process when you can avoid it altogether by making wise choices?

Let's return to King Solomon's graphic description of a sex trap in operation in Proverbs chapter 7. He describes a boy and a girl consumed with physical desire for sexual gratification. It is a story of seduction, sin, and shame in which a prostitute lures a young man to her bedroom for a night of illicit pleasure. Solomon tells us that the boy walked into the trap under his own power.[3]

> *And beheld among the simple ones, I discerned among the youths, a young man void of understanding, passing through the street near her corner; and he went the way to her house, in the twilight, in the evening, in the black and dark night: and, behold, there met him a woman with the attire of an harlot, and subtil of heart* (Proverbs 7:7-10).

This is the house of a prostitute, the house of the *trapper*. Her body and sexual enticements are the bait. The trappee could be *you or me*! The young man in this proverb fell for the bait. He took hold of the cheese and the prostitute said, "Let's go to the trap. Let's do it when it gets dark, when nobody will see us." "And, behold, there met him a woman with the attire of an harlot, and subtil of heart" (Prov. 7:10). She is slick, cunning, and deceitful.

You need to realize just how easy it is for us to cross the line from trappee to trapper. Whether you are a man or a woman, if you are going to minister the Word, you must protect your gift of ministry in your dress and in your social conduct to avoid becoming a stumbling block.

(She is loud and stubborn; her feet abide not in her house: now is she without, now in the streets, and lieth in wait at every corner) (Proverbs 7:11-12).

Some Christian women don't dress like harlots, but they have a harlot spirit. They are loud and stubborn. They don't act like ladies; they act like harlots. They are too bold. If a man so much as takes them out for coffee after choir rehearsal, they will be sitting on his lap on Sunday morning! The spirit of a harlot refuses to change, and she just can't seem to stay home. If you are a woman, when was the last time you spent a whole day by yourself at home? I'm not talking about the mall ministry, or the time you spend at your mama's and Auntie Maybelle's. I'm talking about just you and God at home cheerfully and quietly tending to your life cooking, cleaning, praising, and praying. The Bible says of the harlot, "Now is she without, now in the streets, and lieth in wait at every corner" (Prov. 7:12). She is sent by satan to set people up.

So she caught him, and kissed him, and with an impudent face said unto him, I have peace offerings with me; this day have I payed my vows. Therefore came I forth to meet thee, diligently to seek thy face, and I have found thee. I have decked my bed with coverings of tapestry, with carved works, with fine linen of Egypt. I have perfumed my bed with myrrh, aloes, and cinnamon (Proverbs 7:13-17).

Some people won't blush for any reason. They have no shame. They are bold and brazen. Women have become so aggressive that they will even foot the bill financially for a date. "Brother Jim, would you take me to the church banquet?" "Well, sister, I wasn't really planning..." "Well, if you do, I'll get the car. I've already got the tickets, and I'll even rent you a tuxedo." Young ladies and precious sisters in Christ, something is wrong with this picture. As Christian women, our conduct should reflect Christ. We should challenge ourselves to become ladies of honor, character, and integrity, busy in the Kingdom, "lifting up the name of Jesus." Jesus the living Word declares, "And I, if I be lifted up from the earth, will draw all men unto Me" (Jn. 12:32). If you are an unmarried male or female, if you will just lift up Jesus, then He will draw all men (and women) to Himself. Catch one if you long for a good, godly, hard-working honorable mate!

A harlot will tell a man, "I have been seeking your face (hunting and stalking you). Now I've found you" (from Proverbs 7:15). The enemy may have people out with orders to seduce and destroy you because of the ministry that God has placed in your life. My warning to you is that you had better walk the straight and narrow! Flee from those harlots; steer clear of every evil thing. When Jesus prepared disciples for ministry, He sent them out "by two and two" for their own protection (Mk. 6:7).

The harlot prepares her temptations in advance for the unwary. If you know that there's a dangerous spot in the road, you are a fool if you drive right through it like there's nothing there! "I have decked my bed with coverings of tapestry, with carved works, with fine linen of Egypt. I have perfumed my bed with myrrh, aloes, and cinnamon" (Prov. 7:16-17). A staff pastor went to pray for a sister who was sick, but he want alone against the counsel of the senior pastors. (Remember: Even Jesus sent out His disciples "by two and two.") He assured them that he "knew what he was doing." He opened the door, and that conniving sister was lying on her bed in all of her "how great I am" and feeling remarkably lively. That man barely got out of there (some wonder to this day if he really did).

> *Come, let us take our fill of love until the morning: let us solace ourselves with loves. For the goodman is not at home, he is gone a long journey: he hath taken a bag of money with him, and will come home at the day appointed* (Proverbs 7:18-20).

> *Forbidden appetite* plus *attractive temptation* plus *opportunity in secrecy* will often equal *sin*. This man began falling the moment he looked at the harlot and toyed with her proposition in his mind. You and I are not different—if you play with fire, you are bound to get burned.

> *With her much fair speech she caused him to yield, with the flattering of her lips she forced him. He goeth after her straightway, as an ox goeth to the slaughter, or as a fool to the correction of the stocks; till a dart strike through his liver; as a bird hasteth to the snare, and knoweth not that it is for his life* (Proverbs 7:21-23).

I counsel you to listen carefully to what is not spoken because fair speech and flattering lips can be deadly—especially if they have the appearance of holiness on them. Beware of the man or woman who tells you everything you want to hear, but who isn't doing anything you want him or her to do. "Baby, you know I want to marry you" is *not* the same as "Baby, I will marry you." Don't get the words mixed up. There's a big difference between "want to" and "will."

Some of the most deadly flatterers dress up in "little lamb" costumes and snuggle close to a likely "counselor" and say in mock sadness, "You are so easy to talk to. Could we pray together? You see, my wife never talks to me anymore. Oh, your hair is wonderful. I wish *her* hair looked as good as yours." Put a stop to it. Just tell that lush, "Your wife's hair could look like this if you would give her enough money to go the beauty salon every week like I do." Don't be afraid to challenge and confront a lustful spirit designed to trap you.

More believers need to stand up in the Body of Christ when they encounter a sex trap and say, "Hey, we are family. Now you go home to your wife (or your husband). I am single—but not available. You get right back home to your spouse and do what you need to do to make things right. Go home and stop trying to sweet-talk me, or I'll stand and tell the whole church." Often you must threaten satan with the promise of exposing him and his deceitful works.

"...As a fool to the correction of the stocks; till a dart strike through his liver; as a bird hasteth to the snare, and knoweth not that it is for his life" (Prov. 7:22-23). Thanks to the devil's deceit, most of us don't even know that he is setting us up for death, not a good time. But isn't that the task of deceit—to blind, confuse, or hide the truth?

Hearken unto me now therefore, O ye children, and attend to the words of my mouth. Let not thine heart decline to her ways, go not astray in her paths. For she hath cast down many wounded: yea, many strong men have been slain by her. Her house is the way to hell, going down to the chambers of death (Proverbs 7:24-27).

Solomon also warned us that the spirit of the harlot has "cast down many wounded" (Prov. 7:26). The devil knows when a person is wounded and vulnerable, and he knows that is when people are the most vulnerable to demonic setups. *Satan knows what kind of cheese to put on your trap* during those moments when you are feeling lonely, isolated, forgotten, or abused. A lot of strong Christians and famous Christian leaders have bragged or preached about their chaste lifestyles and their immunity to the devil's lies—but in the end they were brought down to dishonor and sin by both their private pain and their secret lusts.

The hellish harlot's house is the way to hell. The final destination of everyone who lands in a sex trap is hell if something isn't done to rescue them, and if they don't want to be free themselves. You don't just die in the natural either. You will see your dreams and vision die as well, along with your hopes. Your destiny will wither if you remain in a sex trap. Some of us are literally killing our destiny today with the decisions and the choices that we are making. We are even cutting our lives short! When the sicknesses and diseases come upon our body, we will try to say, "Where is God?" as if it is His fault, but it won't work. We have dismissed God's warnings and made wrong choices that landed us in a sex trap. We seized the bait and consumed the pleasure. Now we are crying because the trap has fallen and there seems to be no escape from its consequences.

Endnotes

1. James Strong, *Strong's Exhaustive Concordance of the Bible* (Peabody, Massachusetts: Hendrickson Publishers, n.d.), #H2964, "prey."

2. *Webster's New Universal Unabridged Dictionary*, 2nd ed. (New York: Simon and Schuster, 1983), p. 1717.

3. Mike Murdock, *Wisdom for Winners* (Tulsa, Oklahoma: Honor Books, 1993), p. 142.

Chapter 4

The *Victims* of Sex Traps

During my graduate studies in psychology, I studied the case of a woman who had slept with more than 30 men (unfortunately, this is becoming more common these days). The reason she became the object of psychological study is that she became "schizoid" as a result of her promiscuity. This psychological term is derived from the Greek word *schizo*, which means "to split or sever (literally or figuratively): to break, divide, open, rend, make a rent."[1] This is also the root of the word *schism*, used to describe division in the Church.

Even non-religious psychologists are being forced to recognize that sex isn't so "free" after all. This woman evidently developed schizophrenia, a very serious psychological disorder in which she literally lost her identity and her ability to relate to the real world. By sexually bonding with all her lovers, her own personality became so splintered that she could no longer function as a whole human being in her mind and spirit. Her personality had disintegrated because she was in constant conflict within herself, almost as if all her past lovers were pulling her apart.

I am by no means saying that everyone afflicted with this disorder is guilty of sexual misconduct; however, in this particular case, there seemed to be a very strong "cause and effect" relationship between the victim's promiscuity and her loss of individuality and personality. We were not created to live and mate like dogs, who will join with any available partner with no thought to divine purpose or the consequences of intimacy without commitment and covenant.

The woman in this study had become psychologically (and spiritually) bound to *every man* she had slept with. She was "tied" to every man she "mated." She was in a *sex trap!* The psychological profession would love to find proof that this doesn't really happen, and most non-Christian psychologists would still scoff at the idea of spiritual bonding through sexual intimacy—but that doesn't change the facts. God said it in the Book of Genesis at the dawn of creation, and psychology is being forced to acknowledge the truth stated in the Scriptures:

> *And Adam said, This is now bone of my bones, and flesh of my flesh: she shall be called Woman, because she was taken out of Man. Therefore shall a man leave his father and his mother, and shall cleave unto his wife: and they shall be one flesh* (Genesis 2:23-24).

> *What? know ye not that he which is joined to an harlot is one body? for two, saith He, shall be one flesh* (1 Corinthians 6:16).

Most people don't know it, but a discerning pastor doesn't really have to be told "who is sexually active or 'sleeping' with whom" among wayward members of the flock. If one of them stops sleeping with another and changes partners (as people invariably will, since there is no commitment or covenant to cover human weakness), then whoever was dumped will suddenly find it convenient to reveal what he or she would never confess earlier. Why? There is a built-in sense of possession and ownership involved with sexual intimacy, and it is rooted in the fact that we *give ourselves* in sexual union. We feel that we own what we have invested. That's why God stresses that we are to give ourselves physically and spiritually in marriage and marriage only in the Book of First Corinthians: "Let the husband render unto the wife due benevolence [conjugal duty]: and likewise also the wife unto the husband" (1 Cor. 7:3).

This isn't just our idea—it is another of God's ways of preserving and continually renewing a marriage relationship: "So ought men to *love their wives as their own bodies*. He that loveth his wife loveth himself" (Eph. 5:28). I simply put it like this: "No ringey...no dingey."

Married or not, Sister Red Dress still *feels* married to Brother Fornicator. So when he drops her and picks up Sister Blue Dress, then Sister Red Dress will "tell all" because she is still emotionally and spiritually tied to Brother Fornicator. God made us that way, and no amount of self-justification or antichrist rhetoric can change it.

God never intended for you and I to be tied to the many souls, bodies, and spirits of people. God doesn't want you manipulated and dangled, tossed around, and handled as though you were nothing. (By the way, men are subject to this law too, but they are slower to admit or confront it because of their stronger hormonal drives. However, God holds them even more accountable because they were created to be protectors of women, not predators out to use and destroy women.)

Sin is like a disease. It ruthlessly attacks and destroys everything it comes in contact with until it is stopped. It has no compassion for innocent children, gentle adults, long-standing family relationships, solemn vows, or urgent need.

It has no loyalty to the sinner either. All it knows to do is to consume, distort, disrupt, disturb, and destroy.

When God's law is broken, people suffer. God didn't give us the basic laws of society and the Church to hurt us, but to protect us. No one gets hurt when God's law is followed—the pain always comes when it is broken. If you ever want to grasp the gravity of sin and its consequence, gauge it by the terrible measures God went through to break its grip on the human race. It cost Him the life of His only begotten Son, Jesus Christ.

Sin *always* creates victims. And victims or trappees who are never rescued and healed almost always become trappers like the sinners who hurt them in the first place. Innocent children growing up in abusive homes where one or both adults took out their anger on their children are statistically likely to become angry abusers themselves. The same goes for children of substance abusers, sexual abusers, emotional abusers, and adulterers whose sin breaks up their marriages. Jesus Christ is well able to break all of these circles of destruction of course, but someone somehow must make a stand for righteousness and say, "Enough is enough. I repent."

All the things I have described become even worse (I know it doesn't sound possible) when religious hypocrisy is mixed in with them. Virtually every sin found in the world has found its way into the Church today. We have TV preachers sleeping with choir directors (male and female), respected bishops meeting secret lovers during weeklong out-of-town church conferences, cheat'n deacons flirting with Sunday school teachers, elders meeting with singles for "counseling" at midnight in seedy motel rooms, and model Christian parents sleeping with other model Christian parents from across the street. In the words of James, "My brethren, these things ought not so to be" (Jas. 3:10b).

When Christians sin and end up hurting innocent people around them, they have not only wounded those whom Jesus called "little ones," bringing damnation on their own heads, but they have also stained and destroyed the faith of their victims in the only Source of help and healing that can truly set them free from their pain! Why would a child want to trust "Daddy's God" when Daddy was the one who sexually abused his child in the first place? May God have mercy on their souls—there is going to be a terrible price to pay for those who do not stop, repent, and allow God to deliver.

God doesn't play games like we do. He has *never* been afraid to state His position and take sides in a dispute. He has always been the defender and redeemer of victims. If you don't believe me, then listen to Jesus Himself:

> *And said, Verily I say unto you, Except ye be converted, and become as little children, ye shall not enter into the kingdom of heaven. ... And whoso shall receive one such little child in My name receiveth Me. But whoso shall offend one of these little ones which believe in Me, it were better for him that a millstone were hanged about his neck, and that he were drowned in the depth of the sea. ... Take heed that ye despise not one of these little ones; for I say unto you, That in heaven their angels do always behold the face of My Father which is in heaven. For the Son of man is come to save that which was lost. ... Even so it is not the will of your Father which is in heaven, that one of these little ones should perish* (Matthew 18:3,5-6,10-11,14).

Most of us are far too quick to judge, and too slow to seek the truth, forgive, and extend compassion. We like to throw rocks more than speak words of forgiveness and restoration.

I am amazed every time I read the account of the woman caught in adultery in the eighth chapter of the Gospel of John. If you remember, a woman was dragged in front of Jesus by religious leaders who told Jesus that they had caught her "in the act." Now I don't know about your thoughts on this, but it seems to me that "it takes two to tango." It's strange that only the woman was brought awkward, embarrassed, and naked to Jesus. Where was the "naked" man? Probably somewhere putting his suit back on, getting ready to "preach" or "deacon" again! It also seems to me that when these religious "Bible experts" quoted the Old Testament punishment for adulterers, they left out the part about "both" being punished (see Deut. 22:22-24).

Let me update this scene. The prostitute on your downtown street corner may be "trapping a John" (or customer) today, but she entered this life as an innocent babe. I can almost guarantee you that at some point in her life, whether early or late, she was the victim, a trappee who was used and abused against her will by another. Something caused her to lose her self-esteem and choose the life of a prostitute. Does this justify her ways today? Absolutely not. Does it make it tougher for her to break away from her lifestyle? Yes, without a doubt. A prostitute must not only break free from the power of her sin, but she will almost always have to break away from ruthless men who profit from the sale of her body (pimps), and she has to find a new way to support herself and any dependents. This is a risky venture that can lead to physical violence unless undergirded and guided by the Holy Spirit.

She faces scorn, disdain, and rigid stereotypes both within the world and without. God Himself will move to snap her spiritual yoke, but He generally demands that His Church take up the cross after that to help such a fragile young believer build a new life—even if that means her new spiritual family must underwrite the cost of transplanting her to a new home far away from the street life that once held her. How many churches do you know of that would shoulder a responsibility like that? (God has the same problem—there aren't many.)

Prostitution is one of the most visible types of sex traps. Far more widespread and dangerous is the invisible epidemic of child abuse (sexual, emotional, and physical), and the sexual deviations it can create in its victims. Sexual abuse is the sin that perverts almost everything it touches. Everybody who is sleeping around doesn't necessarily want to. Their normal God-given desires have been perverted by abuse and they need divine help to break free.

Someone somewhere—whether it was an uncle, a daddy, a grandfather, an aunt, a grandmother, or some nasty low-down "church missionary" (my term for male and female sexual predators operating *within* the Church)—got hold of a little girl and perverted her desire to play with little dolls and to make little patty cakes through twisted abuse and misuse. The only way she can fight back and say, "I hate what was done to me," is to grow up and become a prostitute or some other form of sexual predator herself.

You may be tempted to say, "She's fast, she's wild." No. She is hurting. She was the trappee long before she became the trapper. You may be reading this sentence thinking, *I don't want to be like I am either. I don't want to do what I do.* Preachers have called the devil "the enemy of our souls" for good reason. He delights in reducing a woman to the level of thinking, "All I have to offer a man is my body." He likes to make men think of women (and even children) as sex objects that exist only to give them pleasure. The good news is that we have been given victory over the enemy, and that

Jesus wants to lift us out of our pits of bondage. We are not sex objects. We are wonderful beings created in the image of God to bring glory and honor to our Lord. We are people of purpose, promise, and destiny. From our childhood on, we deserve the right to love ourselves, God, and others.

The relationship of parent to child is the most sacred of human relationships apart from the husband/wife relationship. This relationship establishes the boundaries of safety, righteousness, and danger in a child's life. God charges the parents with the job of modeling true manhood and womanhood before their children. The natural result of this is that, instinctively, the child will seek out a mate of the opposite sex who has the characteristics of his or her first and most trusted role model—the parent of the opposite sex.

Most of our serious sexual problems stem from deviations, failures, or problems in the parent-child relationship. This explains why satan works overtime to victimize young children—particularly at the hands of their fathers, the chief authority figure and chief protector in their lives. Without exception, this puts children at greater risk of sexual deviation and confusion throughout their lives.

I see a vicious cycle churning through the church ranks, and it is only perpetuated by our tendency to "push it under the rug" and pretend that sexual deviations don't exist in our churches. Let me assure you that they do, and that they have reached the epidemic stage. God says, "Enough!" I am convinced that He is about to bring wonderful deliverance to those who have been snared by satan and want to be free! Jesus can and will undo the works of satan.

I am tired of pretenders and assenters. It's time to tell the truth and call sin what it is: *sin*. The Church is riddled with what I call "temple sluts, whores, and prostitutes" sent by satan to set traps in the Kingdom. There are women who are lesbians who actively recruit sexual partners or lay traps for heterosexual women in the church. This is a sex trap, and I'm going to call it what it is—no matter who blushes or protests. We've got too many "missionaries" who hunt for younger vulnerable women and say, "I just want to be your mama." I caution young ladies and parents throughout the world to be on the alert. God has not designated all these so-called "god-relationships," whether these predators call themselves god-sisters, god-brothers, or god-mothers. Beware of these *sex traps*!

One woman came up to me in a meeting who was hugging me just a little tighter than she should have. She kept trying to touch me the wrong way, so I got in her face and said in language she could understand, "Sister girl, you really don't know me. I am a fool for God. Now if you keep this up, I will kill you and tell God that you died! Just pull yourself away from me. Don't make the mistake of thinking that because I like to touch and hug people that I am some kind of lesbian. I am into men—not into women. Don't press your 'bumper lumpers' up against my 'lumpers.' " (I am going into detail because somebody reading this book needs the blunt truth to be set free. I'm willing to take some criticism if it will break the devilish bondage over somebody's life.)

It is said that homosexuals far outnumber lesbians, and that their aggressiveness and lust can be shocking. Contrary to satan's lie in the secular world, homosexuals aren't born like that. They might have been abused at such a young age that they assumed they were "that way" all their lives, but God is well able to restore their true masculinity. Most homosexuals have been terribly hurt, abused, or disappointed by the male father figure in their lives. In many cases, domineering mothers played into the picture with a smothering love that made females unattractive mates, while their approval was nevertheless needed for happiness and self-worth.

If you are in the sex trap of homosexuality, then it is time for you to understand that God has healing and deliverance just for you. A real man is created to fulfill *God's definition* of manhood. Homosexuals will always be incomplete men until they repent of their sin and ask God to heal the pain within. He will restore the true purpose of manhood to them. There are too many women competing for too few real men already. We don't have time for men to be crossing over. If you were born a man, we need you to be a man according to God's plan.

A wonderful man of God named Joe Dallas has written an anointed book entitled, *Desires in Conflict*.[2] This book is a powerful ministry tool that declares there is "real hope for those who struggle with homosexuality" and the people who love them. Dallas says, "The conflicts are real." The most prominent conflicts include (a) the desire to love God versus the desire to be loved in a way God prohibits; (b) the desire for a normal sex life versus the desire to satisfy feelings that seem normal but aren't; and (c) the desire to be transparent versus the desire to avoid the pain of misunderstanding.

Although there is no quick fix, there is effective help for restoring sexual wholeness and moving ahead in one's Christian life. Dallas says, "Probably most important in understanding deliverance from homosexuality (including lesbianism) is that there is '*no quick fix*.' Homosexuality doesn't just vanish when a person decides he or she doesn't want it."[3] One must be willing to go through a process of growth rather than expect a "microwave-quick" change.

Andy Comiskey, the founder and director of Desert Stream Ministries in Santa Monica, California, and the author of

Pursuing Sexual Wholeness, once lectured that "We are the people of the immediate." The microwave has usurped the stove, automated tellers keep us out of the bank lines, and liposuction is so much snappier than dieting. Convenience is everything. We resent waiting. Well, when one wants deliverance from homosexuality, this mentality is lethal. It has led many people to try shock treatment, exorcism, and sexual experimentation with the opposite sex in hopes of a quick cure. Joe Dallas reports that the results are always the same: "failure and disillusionment."[4]

Why? Because homosexuality—including lesbianism—is not one isolated "trap" or problem. It is symptomatic of other problems that are deeply ingrained and often hard to detect. Like a red light on an automobile dashboard, it indicates that something under the hood needs to be checked. Scripture bears this out. In the Book of Romans, the apostle Paul describes homosexual passions as a result of something deeper:

> *Because that, when they knew God, they glorified Him not as God, neither were thankful; but...their foolish heart was darkened. ... For this cause God gave them up unto vile affections: for even their women did change the natural use into that which is against nature: and likewise also the men, leaving the natural use of the woman, burned in their lust one toward another; men with men working that which is unseemly, and receiving in themselves that recompence of their error which was meet* (Romans 1:21,26-27).

Joe Dallas reveals that "aside from condemning homosexual lust, Paul is pointing out its symptomatic nature. The real problem cited here is universal sin, of which homosexuality is but a symptom. Thus, the homosexual orientation is caused by other factors and they, not just the sexual attractions, need to be dealt with."[5]

Although the sex trap of homosexuality is complex, there are a few principles that will always hold true. "On the authority of the Bible, we can state that homosexuality is unnatural and contrary to God's intention for sexual experience, and that homosexual acts are always—without exception—immoral. There is no such thing as a 'typical' homosexual, there is no one reason people become homosexual, and there is no one method of dealing with homosexuality."[6]

One thing rings true, however. As you begin the walk of sanctification, no changes can occur, no growth can be obtained, unless the foundation of integrity is laid through repentance, discipline, and commitment. This is true in every area of life, but it is doubly true when dealing with sexuality. Once your foundation of integrity is laid, you must seek to "get out and stay out" of your trap through:[7]

1. the maintenance of sexual integrity,

2. the courage to face and confront relationships and patterns that are unhealthy,

3. the search for the "perfect parent,"

4. the establishment of healthy and nonsexual friendships, and

5. acknowledging and working through problems of childhood, trauma, emotional dependency, and gender identity.

Many would argue, "But isn't faith in Christ enough to correct this problem? Aren't we born again? Are not all things made new, as Paul said? (2 Cor. 5:17) Isn't God sufficient to deliver us from any problems we have—including homosexuality?" Joe Dallas says "yes" to all these questions, but he would add that God has created us with emotional needs that, by His design, can only be satisfied through people.

It was God, after all, who looked at Adam and said, "It is not good for man to be alone" (see Gen. 2:18). Adam already enjoyed the intimate fellowship of God, but God Himself declared that man needed something more. It is argued that the trap of homosexuality is a relational problem having its roots in some relational deficit between parent and child, between a child and other children, or between the person and other people in general. Since homosexuality is a problem generated by faulty relationships, Joe Dallas suggests that its solution may be found in healthy relationships. Salvation, which secures our eternal relationship with God, is only the beginning of emotional health.

When we, as a result of our salvation and the benefits that come with it, begin to experience human intimacy as God intended us to, then we find healing for damaged emotions, faulty self-perceptions, and unsatisfied longings. It's not that faith in Christ isn't enough; instead, faith in Christ is the beginning.

I want to speak to everyone in this trap. I've been blessed by the writings and ministry of Joe Dallas, the president of Exodus International. He boldly reminds you that you are not "gay"; you are not a "faggot" or a "recovering homosexual." You are not an "ex-gay" or even a "straight wannabe." What you are is a fighter!

"You are fighting an internal battle with desires you didn't ask for and are most likely trying to resist. You're fighting against the misunderstanding that so many people have about those in your position. You are fighting the urge to throw up your hands in despair, to give up, to give in. You're fighting to survive, and you're fighting to win."[8]

Keep fighting the good fight of faith. Keep fighting, for you are "more than a conqueror" (see Rom. 8:37). You can win! One day you will look back at the bait and the trap that held you in bondage, crippled you, and tried to take your very life, and you will say, "Thank You, Lord, for perfecting everything that concerns me..." (see Ps. 138:8).

You need to know that God created you to be a wonderful hometown hero. God didn't make Adam and Steve, He made Adam and Eve. The women need you and you need the women of God. You need to come out of that trap of homosexuality. You can and you will!

I come against the lying spirit that tells you, "You have been in it too long—you can't get out now." Let me tell you, "Nothing that you are going through is too filthy, too nasty, too dirty, too private, and too secret for Jesus to reveal and heal. He was hung up for your hang-ups! He already knows what you are going through and He took care of it on Calvary." Don't let the devil tell you that you have been in it too long. Just tell him, "You can get out and stay out!"

How Do I Get Out?

Coming out hurts because it involves changes. And change hurts. You can make the right choices and get out of your sex trap today. But right choices and right changes can only occur if you have the right information. God says, "My people are destroyed for lack of knowledge..." (Hos. 4:6). Knowledge provides understanding and understanding motivates us to make right judgments so we can make right decisions. I didn't write this book as some kind of academic exercise. The world's libraries are filled with academic exercises, but they didn't do a thing to help people fulfill their divine destiny. *This ain't one of them.* I'm writing this book for only two reasons: First, God told me to. Second, I'm interested in seeing you or your loved ones delivered from sex traps today! You don't have to look any further for my motives. In the name of Jesus, I want to see you released from your trap.

You may not realize it, but most sex traps don't even concern sex. They have to do with satan's attempts to steal or sever your relationship with God. He tries to destroy and deplete your deepest needs and usher in guilt, fear, worry, doubt, and unbelief. Sex traps are just another satanic tool or device to bring about your destruction, and you need to be wise to them. As Paul said, "Lest Satan should get an advantage of us: for we are not ignorant of his devices" (2 Cor. 2:11).

Sex traps have been some of satan's most powerful tools and he has used them from the beginning of human history to bring down or hamper some of our most gifted men and women (including but not limited to King David, Absalom, Solomon, Abraham, Noah, and Samson).

The Spirit of the living God has brought you to this book to bring light to your darkness, and hope to your despair. He is ready and able to arrest the powers of satan, and loose you and set you free! I'm declaring to you in the power of God: *You don't have to be who the devil says you are!* It is time for you to discover what God says about you:

I will praise Thee; for I am fearfully and wonderfully made: marvellous are Thy works; and that my soul knoweth right well (Psalm 139:14).

The Lord will perfect that which concerneth me: Thy mercy, O Lord, endureth for ever: forsake not the works of Thine own hands (Psalm 138:8).

Nay, in all these things we are more than conquerors through Him that loved us (Romans 8:37).

For He hath made Him to be sin for us, who knew no sin; that we might be made the righteousness of God in Him (2 Corinthians 5:21).

Endnotes

1. James Strong, *Strong's Exhaustive Concordance of the Bible* (Peabody, Massachusetts: Hendrickson Publishers, n.d.) #G4977, "schism."

2. Published through Harvest House Publishers.

3. Joe Dallas, *Desires in Conflict* (Eugene, Oregon: Harvest House Publishers, 1991), p. 8.

4. Dallas, *Desires in Conflict*, p. 9.

5. Dallas, *Desires in Conflict*, p. 10.

6. Dallas, *Desires in Conflict*, p. 10.

7. Dallas, *Desires in Conflict*, p. 11.

8. Dallas, *Desires in Conflict*, pp. 12-13.

Chapter 5

It's the Bait That Seals Your Fate

The most effective traps in the natural world use *bait* to lure their prey into harm's way. Bait is a carefully prepared deceit, it is death on a stick, an enticement engineered to speak to a corresponding hunger or appetite. It leads one from freedom to bondage. It smells good. It looks good. It feels good, and it tastes good—but it is connected to a deadly trap. In his book, *Can You Stand to Be Blessed?* Bishop T.D. Jakes describes the power of attractions to lure us:

> "Attractions are allurements that can be based on memories, past experiences, and early associations. It is therefore very difficult to explain the extremely sensitive and fragile feelings that cause us to be attracted. Suffice it to say that we are instinctively attracted to inner needs. That attraction may be based upon a need to be with someone whom we think is attractive, which creates within us a certain validation of our own worth, or the attraction may be based on a deeper, less physical value. *Either way, need is the fuel that spawns attraction*" (emphasis mine).[1]

What does God say about *sex traps* and sin? God loves us so much that He sent His only begotten Son to die so we might have liberty from the bondage of sin. His only requirement is that we love Him in the same way that He loves us. Israel failed repeatedly. For years and years, hundreds of years, God suffered their disobedience. Finally, after many attempts to get their attention, God fulfilled His warning in the Book of Leviticus:

Ye shall make you no idols nor graven image, neither rear you up a standing image, neither shall ye set up any image of stone in your land, to bow down unto it: for I am the Lord your God. ... But if ye will not hearken unto Me, and will not do all these commandments; and if ye shall despise My statutes, or if your soul abhor My judgments, so that ye will not do all My commandments, but that ye break My covenant: I also will do this unto you; I will even appoint over you terror, consumption.... And I will destroy your high places, and cut down your images, and cast your carcases upon the carcases of your idols, and My soul shall abhor you (Leviticus 26:1,14-16,30).

God has also led the way for each of us to come out of the bondage of sin through salvation. He liberated us, and because of the finished work of Jesus Christ on Calvary, sin no longer has the right to be our master. We have been freed from its control because Jesus Christ has led us out of our own personal "Egypts."

*Knowing this, that our old man is crucified with Him [Jesus], that the body of sin might be destroyed, **that henceforth we should not serve sin.** For he that is dead is freed from sin. Now if we be dead with Christ, we believe that we shall also live with Him: knowing that Christ being raised from the dead dieth no more; death hath no more dominion over Him. For in that He died, He died unto sin once: but in that He liveth, He liveth unto God. Likewise reckon ye* *also yourselves to be dead indeed unto sin, but alive unto God through Jesus Christ our Lord* (Romans 6:6-11).

Now He expects us to put Him first in our lives by loving Him most. Anything that we put before Him in this life becomes an idol, just as real as the wooden and stone images that the Israelites erected on hilltops thousands of years ago.

Have you ever wondered why the Israelites put up those high places of idolatry after all the great things God had done for them? Why did they disobey God? Why didn't they do what God asked them to do? We know from the Scriptures that they chose over and over again to act disobediently, knowing full well that they would have to suffer the consequences. Does this sound vaguely familiar?

Bishop Jakes again has some powerful insights into the power of attractions and the needs that trigger them in our lives:

> "Attractions, for many people, can be as deadly as a net to a fish. Seemingly, they can't see that the net is a trap until it is too late. They struggle, trying to get away, but the more they struggle, the more entangled they become. Like drug addicts, they make promises they can't keep, trying to pull away from something that holds them in its grasp like a vice. The key is not to struggle with the thing or person. The deliverance comes from within and not from without. God is far too wise to put your deliverance in the hands of someone or something that may not have any compassion for you. The victory is won within the battleground of your mind, and its memories and needs."[2]

I've lost count of the young women in churches, involved in sexual relationships, who have told me, "Well, he wants to get married, but I *don't!*" I confess that I'll never understand their reasoning. There are thousands of women who are fasting and praying for a man who is willing to make a lifelong commitment in marriage! Yet when these young women have a chance to be holy, upright, and modest through marriage to a man they love—they buy the world's line of promiscuous selfishness and say, "I don't want to get married. I want to be free to live my own life." I just want to shake them and say, "What's the matter with you? Why don't you want to be married? Are you going to be celibate the rest of your life? It is women like you who make it hard on the rest of us!"

I know only one way to minister the Word—and that is direct and to the point. I tell women—even in mixed audiences—the hard truth about their sexual antics:

> "God put a high price tag on you—*it should cost a man a lifetime commitment* to enjoy your sexual favors. Everybody who is offering 'free goodies' should close up shop and put their clothes back on. They should put on a jogging suit plus a dress if they have to, but they need to start telling those men: 'No! No sex without marriage. No! We are holy women.' If more women would respond this way, I tell you, we wouldn't have the problems we have today."

Look again at the prophetic passage in Psalm 124 that we examined in Chapter 3:

> *Blessed be the Lord, who hath not given us as a prey to their teeth. Our soul is escaped as a bird out of the snare of the fowlers: the snare is broken, and we are escaped. Our help is in the name of the Lord, who made heaven and earth* (Psalm 124:6-8).

Now this passage tells us that: (a) God didn't give us to be prey, (b) that our soul is escaped out of the snare, (c) that the snare is broken and we are free, and (d) that our help is in the name of the Lord. Why do we need help from the name of our Lord if the snare or the trap that was set for our destruction has been broken and we are free? Doesn't that same Scripture say that we weren't given to be prey, that our soul is escaped out of the snare, and that the snare is broken and we are free? Then why does the psalmist go on to tell us that our help is in the name of the Lord? It is because we need the Lord's ever-present help to keep our souls free, and to set our bodies and bodily appetites free from the old attractions.

We need the Lord's help to destroy the broken snares and traps in our lives so satan can't put them back together to catch us again. Why do you think Paul wrote these words?

But the Lord is faithful, who shall stablish you, and keep you from evil. And we have confidence in the Lord touching you, that ye both do and will do the things which we command you. And the Lord direct your hearts into the love of God, and into the patient waiting for Christ. Now we command you, brethren, in the name of our Lord Jesus Christ, that ye withdraw yourselves from every brother that walketh disorderly, and not after the tradition which he received of us (2 Thessalonians 3:3-6).

Have you ever been delivered from a trap, and then before you knew it found yourself hanging around that trap again, smelling for the "cheese" you continually crave? It doesn't matter whether your addiction is for American cheese, cheddar cheese, blue cheese, or Farmer's cheese—it is still a deadly addiction meant to entrap you again. The devil knows what cheese to grab you with. You may be one of the thousands of people reading this book who have truly been set free from a deadly addiction—yet you continue to linger around the broken traps of your past because they still contain the bait that your mind, emotions, and fleshly appetites crave.

Sooner or later, someone from satanic territory will show up to put that trap back together again. It may be a hideous imp, a demon, or a delightful but sin-filled memory. Maybe the devil will just "freshen the bait" by sending along a familiar face from forbidden territory, a wrong associate or illicit friendship that will pull you back into the sex trap again. Before you know it, you will be caught again. Locked, blocked, crushed, and tied, you've fallen back into satan's sex trap. That is why if you know you need to be separated from every hint of your addiction, then you need to separate yourself. T.D. Jakes illustrates the need to break devilish control in this way:

> "My children have a remote control toy car. The remote is designed so the car can be controlled even from a distance. The reason we can control the car by an external item is the small apparatus inside the car that is affected by the remote control. If we remove the inner apparatus, the remote control will not work. It is the same way with attractions. They evolve and manipulate us only because there is some inner apparatus that makes us vulnerable to them. If the wrong person, place, or thing controls our remote, we are in trouble. We may not be able to stop the person from playing with the buttons, but we can remove the inner apparatus."[3]

God says that when you can't destroy the enemy in your life, change locations. Only God has the power to destroy satan or remove him from this earth. Our only recourse is to stay away from the places that belong to him. If we are hanging out at the devil's bar, and we're not really there to conduct "seize and rescue" operations on lost souls, then we are on his territory and we have no authority there because we are "AWOL" (absent without leave). If you are out of your area of jurisdiction without God's permission, then you can quote, command, and demand all you want to and the devil won't move. He doesn't have to obey rebels because they belong to him.

If you cannot get the demon away from you, then move yourself away from the demon! If drinking is your problem and they won't close the bar on the corner, *move!* Don't hold a revival in a bar if you know you like wine. Why? Because before the revival is over, that wine will find its way back into your life in a revival of sin. Get to know yourself. Learn to recognize your weaknesses and cravings. For instance, I know that I like wine. When I was pregnant with my first child, the doctor told me to take a tablespoon of wine every night to build up the iron levels in my blood. Boy, was I grateful! After I delivered my baby, I told him, "Check my blood, Doc. Ain't it still a little low?" That told me that Wanda likes wine a little too much. I can't hang around it. I have no business conducting a revival in a bar because I might stumble out of that meeting drunk.

You know what kind of bait will snag you and drag you into the devil's trap. You know what makes your toes curl. You know that certain member of the opposite sex in your church who is married—and you also know that every time you see that person you suddenly feel "led" to work on that person's committee! Now if you know that person isn't available and you aren't available, then you have no business getting on that person's committee. Volunteer for the prayer chain instead and meet with other believers of your own sex for prayer at 5 o'clock in the morning. Just remove yourself from temptation with a healthy dose of wisdom and common sense. You need to be delivered from your addiction, and you know exactly what you want on your personal sex trap.

Now remember that a trap is an apparatus or a device designed to ensnare or hold you until death. It is not there just to "catch you"; it was designed to kill you! The largest spring traps have teeth in them that are designed to rip you apart if you try to escape before you bleed to death. Don't think that the enemy will let you see the trap first—he knows you are too smart for a direct attack. That's why he lets you smell, feel, or look at the bait first. The devil knows whether you like Swiss cheese, American cheese, cheddar cheese, or jalapeno cheese. You have one guess about what he will use to bait your trap. If you are saying, "But everywhere I look, I see the thing I want," if you can't get the trap away from you, get away from the trap. The problem is that we want what that bait offers, and we think that we can be slick enough to get the cheese and miss the trap. That's called deceit. David, Solomon, and Samson weren't that good and neither are you.

Every time you smell your favorite cheese on those traps, remember what lies hidden under, around, or above the cheese. There is a hidden trap waiting to slam down on your life. The devil doesn't just want to hurt you; he is out for your life. He is out for your relationship with God. And let me assure you that preachers are not exempt! If anything, their prominence makes them a juicier target. As I mentioned earlier, God told me that "somebody has to change the dirty diapers from the pulpit to the pew." That means preachers and bishops are not exempt. First ladies in the local church are not exempt. Missionaries are not exempt. Convention-goers and seminar-seekers are not exempt.

When I first began to tell young ladies around the country to tell their men, "No ringey, no dingey," I was a happily married woman with "some dingey at home." I had somebody lying on my pillow, and it was legal. I had spiritual rights and sexual privileges as a wife of 24 years. But when the man died and the pillow was replaced with a teddy bear, I began to wonder if I really believed in the "no ringey, no dingey" idea.

I was a widow, but I was still a woman with the same drives and desires I had when I shared my bed with a husband for 24 years. The "urge to merge" didn't vanish at the funeral service. However, you have to *give God permission* to "zip you up, and tie you up." When I began to let my thoughts wander, God pulled my chain real quick and reminded me of the consequences of those thoughts. Were my desires for companionship wrong? Absolutely not. Bishop T.D. Jakes writes,

> "We are communal by nature; we have a strong need for community and relationships. However, whatever we are in relationship with, we also are related to. It is important that we do not covenant with someone or something with which we are not really related....we are forbidden from seeking intimacy, which is a legitimate need, from an inappropriate source. This is a biological law that governs biological order [referring to Genesis 1:24-25]...

> "What was introduced in the shadow of the Old Testament theology as a biological law is magnified in the New Testament as a spiritual reality...Now it is

not biologically illegal for us to bond with unbelievers; *it is spiritually illegal*...The central concept is to avoid intimate contact with dead things."[4]

I want to take this one step further. As women in the Body of Christ, we must also harness our desires to cook, clean, shop, and baby-sit for men in the Kingdom who have not committed themselves to marriage! All too often, we make life too easy for the single men in our churches. We should not be sharing houses, cars, children, or budgets outside of the marriage covenant. Soon, you will be sharing physical intimacy—outside of marriage and outside of God's blessing. We must remember: "No ringey, no dingey."

One of the keys to overcoming the attraction of the sex traps littering our path and our past is found in the Book of Jude:

> *But ye, beloved,* **building up yourselves on your most holy faith, praying in the Holy Ghost, keep yourselves in the love of God,** *looking for the mercy of our Lord Jesus Christ unto eternal life. And of some have compassion, making a difference: and others save with fear, pulling them out of the fire; hating even the garment spotted by the flesh. Now unto* **Him that is able to keep you from falling, and to present you faultless** *before the presence of His glory with exceeding joy, to the only wise God our Saviour, be glory and majesty, dominion and power, both now and ever. Amen* (Jude 20-25).

Endnotes

1. T.D. Jakes, *Can You Stand to Be Blessed?* (Shippensburg, Pennsylvania: Treasure House, 1997), p. 65. Used by permission.

2. Jakes, *Can You Stand to Be Blessed?*, p. 66.
3. Jakes, *Can You Stand to Be Blessed?*, p. 67.
4. Jakes, *Can You Stand to Be Blessed?*, pp. 68, 71.

Chapter 6

The Direction of Your Desire Is Important

Desire is a gift from God. I said this in an earlier chapter, but it bears repeating. Desire only becomes evil when it is twisted by deceit into a lustful obsession for sheer physical gratification without fear, respect, or regard for God or His Word. "Desire is good or bad based on the direction that it takes."[1] Do not believe the old lie that if you pray long enough, read the Bible enough, sing well, and fast two or three times a week, that you won't be bothered by sexual desire.

If satan can get you to believe a lie, then you will begin to speak and act in line with that lie. The Word of God declares, "Thou art snared with the words of thy mouth" (Prov. 6:2a). A modern interpretation would be, "What you say is what you get." If you speak the eternal truths of God, then you will walk in His truth and enjoy the fruits of God's truth. If you buy the lie that the devil speaks to you about your desires, then you will start speaking that lie, and you will begin to act it out.

The enemy loves to play with our desires. He will alternate between two equally outrageous lies just to jar you and

---

badger you into yielding to sin for the sake of self. Before he can walk you into a *sex trap*, he will usually wear you down over time and then tell you, "Why struggle any longer? Everybody else is doing it." If you say, "Everybody else is *not* doing it," then he will move on to the next lie.

He will prompt the spirit or mind of the person who is trying to lure you into the sex trap to pull out what has to be the second-oldest lie in history: "You would if you *really* loved me." (The first lie of satan in Genesis 3:1 was, "Did God *really say*...." He is still whispering, "*Did He really mean it?*")

One way to answer the second-oldest lie in history is to say, "Hey, I don't have to try on the shoe and wear it for a week before I take the money to the store and pay for it. I don't have to prove to you that I love you by lying down with you sexually before I marry you. You need to *prove to me* that you love me for who I am instead of for what I can give you. Prove to me that I am worth waiting for, or show yourself to the door and lock it on the way out."

Unfortunately, this problem isn't restricted to men who are trying to entice women into sexual sin. There are a lot of women out there who shamelessly say, "Show me that you're a man." Mister, you need to tell that Jezebel, "Woman, I'm not going to show you anything. Every time I step out of my shower I know who I am. I wouldn't give up my salvation just to prove the obvious to somebody like you."

"Desire plays a big role in getting you into or out of satan's sex traps."[2] That is why the direction of your desire is important. There are two men in the Bible whose lives perfectly picture the consequences of the direction of their desires.

Samson was a good-looking, massively built hero of Israel who had everything going for him. This boy was raised in a godly home and he lived a set-apart life with a clear destiny for his life. The miraculous power of God followed him from childhood right into manhood. He had made a secret vow that God chose to make the final barrier he was never to cross (kind of a repeat of the forbidden tree in the garden).

But Samson had a problem that he didn't deal with. He lusted for things he wasn't supposed to have. He had a special weakness for women from the race that dominated his own people. He was engaged to a Philistine woman and then saw her given to another. He went into a Philistine harlot and almost fell into a trap. Then he fell in love with the wrong woman in the valley of Sorek. In his pride, Samson didn't realize that his supernatural physical strength didn't necessarily cover the spiritual weakness revealed in his sexual desire for ungodly women.

> *And it came to pass afterward, that he loved a woman in the valley of Sorek, whose name was Delilah. And the lords of the Philistines came up unto her, and said unto her, Entice him, and see wherein his great strength lieth, and by what means we may prevail against him, that we may bind him to afflict him: and we will give thee every one of us eleven hundred pieces of silver* (Judges 16:4-5).

It is easy to over-spiritualize things sometimes, but the woman whom Samson fell for has too many coincidences to ignore. This woman was in the "valley of Sorek," which in the Hebrew might be translated as "in the narrow valley of choice red wine"[3] or "the good stuff." It really gets interesting when you realize the contrast between the names of this classic odd couple from Bible times. While Samson's Hebrew name, *Shimshown*, meant "sunlight," his girlfriend's name, Delilah, meant "languishing; to slacken or be feeble; figuratively, to be oppressed:—bring low, dry up, be emptied, be not equal, fail, be impoverished, be made thin."[4] She sounds like the perfect match for God's champion, doesn't she? Satan obviously thought so.

This is a perfect picture of the sex traps that satan lays for God's men and women every day across the world. Our ancient enemy wants to find the secret weakness in us that will bring us down. As he did with Samson centuries ago, the devil excels at finding our "perfect destructive match" and using them to use our *desires* against us. Samson fell right into satan's trap even quicker because of pride. He liked to "play" and show off his gift from God. (Too many men and women of God "play" with the powerful gifts that God has placed in their lives. This can easily become a snare through pride, and a weak point that gives satan a place of entrance into their lives.)

The direction your desire takes will determine whether you are going to be blessed or cursed. Samson ran right into the arms of the wrong woman and it cost the man named "Sunlight" any chance of ever seeing sunlight again. He literally lost his namesake through unchecked, ungodly desires. He aimed his hormones toward the pit and plowed right in.

Joseph, on the other hand, dealt with desire in a totally different way. While Samson enjoyed the company of immorality and death, Joseph delighted himself in the Lord and got a promotion. Your promotion in God may hinge on the direction of your desire! Double-check the direction of your desire if you are looking for God to take you higher, or want God to take your ministry to a new level. Carefully aim your desires if you are looking for a promotion in the natural or perhaps a new station in life or even new finances.

Joseph *didn't* have everything going for him when he was confronted by the wrong woman. The youngest son in his family, he was rejected and betrayed by his brothers and abandoned to a hopeless life of slavery in a foreign land. Yet the one thing he did have, and the one thing he clung to no matter where he found himself each day, was the dreams he had received from God.

His first place of service as a slave was in the household of Potiphar, the chief of Pharaoh's guard. This was a man you didn't want to cross. He would rank somewhere between the Secretary of Defense and the Director of the FBI in our day. Joseph quickly proved his ability as an administrator and won Potiphar's confidence and trust. Unfortunately, Joseph also caught the eye of Potiphar's lustful wife.

> And it came to pass after these things, that his master's wife cast her eyes upon Joseph; and she said, Lie with me. ... And it came to pass, as she spake to Joseph day by day, that he hearkened not unto her, to lie by her, or to be with her. ... And she caught him by his garment, saying, Lie with me: and he left his garment in her hand, and fled, and got him out (Genesis 39:7,10,12).

What will you do with your desire? You have a choice. Either you will run away from what God has forbidden, or you will run to lay your head in sin's deadly lap. Joseph chose to *run* from Potiphar's wife and he won the victory though he was unjustly punished for a time. Sometimes when you do right you will suffer for it. But suffer anyway. If you suffer with the Lord, you will reign with the Lord (see 2 Tim. 2:12). The apostle Paul echoed Joseph's choice in his warning to young Timothy and those whom he pastored: "Flee also youthful lusts: but follow righteousness, faith, charity, peace, with them that call on the Lord out of a pure heart" (2 Tim. 2:22).

Sometimes things are made much worse because married women in the Body of Christ set up their men for adultery when they stop running to their husbands for affection, intimacy, and love. Samson was a man of God, and he ran too. Delilah is every married woman's nightmare and every man's fantasy. She was the kind of woman who could make a man give up a kingdom. We may not respect Delilah for her morals, but she must have been some kind of woman, and she knew what she was doing! So if you are a wise wife, you will study Delilah and see what it took to get that man's head in her lap.

When temptation comes, will your desire take the wrong direction and run into a trap like Samson ran to Delilah, or will you go the right direction and flee from the trap like Joseph did with Potiphar's wife?

Don't think it was easy for Joseph to say no and run. It wasn't. When Joseph ran from that woman, he ran from somebody who represented a real temptation. Potiphar's wife was probably a beautiful woman. She wasn't ugly. (And by the law of that day, Potiphar had the power to order Joseph's death.) When was the last time you were tested and tried? Too many of us are quick to condemn others when we have never been tested and tried ourselves.

You never know when you will be faced with a decision to go the way of Joseph or the way of Samson. I was ministering in the Midwest recently and after the service I went to the hotel room to relax. Naturally I turned on the TV and began looking for the Christian Broadcasting Network, Trinity Broadcasting, or a local Christian station. I was flipping through the channels with the remote control when I suddenly saw something that made me stop and stare. I said, "Oh my. I didn't know you could do that like that."

I turned off the TV and called my husband. "Honey, you won't believe what I saw on TV," I said. "I didn't know people did that to each other like that." Andrew told me, "That's how people get caught in pornography. It's just as simple as looking. The devil really is alive." Well, I hung up the phone and turned the TV back on. Of course I began looking for the Christian station again, and do you know where I landed again? Once again I stopped and stared and said in proper indignation, "Oh my God. Look what they are doing now!" Do you know that if I had continued to watch that program, that it could have planted a seed of corruption in my memory in just 30 to 60 seconds?

Just give the devil a second and he can change your life. That's why you can't give him *any time*. There is a song lyric that says something like, "If you let him ride, he'll want to drive." You can't let the devil in your life. If you start reading and watching filthy things, then it is almost inevitable that you will one day begin to act them out in your own life.

Christians who have allowed lusts to take hold in their lives are easy to spot. Almost any lady in the Body of Christ can tell you of the times they have felt like a "brother" in the church undressed them with his eyes. There are men who can say the same thing has happened to them under the bold stares of women (or men). It doesn't mean any of these victims were being fast or flirty. It doesn't have to do with whether we are pretty or beautiful—the act was motivated by the lustful spirit that has captured the hearts of the other individuals. They don't know when to turn it off, so they come to church and it exposes them.

Many times, women get caught up in the lusty lifestyles of the rich and famous (and godless) on the soap opera circuit. They consume lustful novels by the boxful, fill their minds with juicy talk at the beauty parlor, and then carry those same lusts into the church and direct their desire toward the most prominent man in the church building—the pastor. Ladies, may I tell you something? I don't care how anointed Pastor DoGood becomes, he is not going to marry you. Don't come to church with that spirit of lust, and don't plan to wait around for Sister DoGood to die off or move away suddenly. She is well, she is healthy, and she isn't going anywhere. God's Word warns us, "Touch not Mine anointed, and do My prophets no harm" (1 Chron. 16:22).

God is not amused or pleased when you slide up beside your married pastor and whisper, "Pastor, could I see you? I know the Lord has given you such a big vision, and He has moved over me to help you in your vision. I have lots of money. You just tell me how much you need." I rebuke you in the name of the Lord Jesus. Just drop your money in the offering plate and run to the altar to repent of your sin.

Men in particular are tempted by satan to direct their desire toward the innocent and the helpless. The strength of their sexual drive, originally designed to ensure the future of the race, can whirl out of control in frightening ways when satan's lies are accepted as truth. One of satan's most twisted attacks on man's natural instinct to tenderly protect and preserve children involves pedophilia. This is the sin of an adult, usually a man, who acts out his sex traps on children. It has become such a scourge in the Church that you've got to screen every potential church employee and get liability insurance on everyone who works in any children's ministry or church day care! These men usually operate with a spirit of fear by threatening their victims after they abuse them. Countless numbers of adults in the Body of Christ are still scarred by what someone did to them as a child.

Right now, I come against that spirit and I go all the way back *to when you were a little boy and a little girl. If you were damaged by abuse, I break that power of satan over your life. I loose you from that pain, from that perversion. I set you free in the name of the Lord Jesus!*

Satan also entices men and women into bestiality (sexual activity with animals). This was even forbidden in the law of Moses, because it was a common sin found among pagan religions rooted in demon worship. And today, God still forbids the mixing of man with animal.

By far, the most common attack on godly masculinity is homosexuality, as we mentioned in Chapter 4. In every case, we each face a choice. How and where will we direct our desire? If we go God's way, He will provide guidance, abundance, strength, and the ability to stand in His holiness. If we go the way of Samson and run to satisfy our desires outside of God's perfect provision, then we will reap the consequences. We live in bold times because the devil knows these are the endtimes. He works overtime to catch, ensnare, and entrap us. Don't let him do it to you. Get smart. Get in the Word and don't let the devil trap you.

The Book of Proverbs tells the promiscuous man, "And thou [will] mourn at the last, when thy flesh and thy body are consumed" (Prov. 5:11). The Bible may well be talking about an assortment of sexually transmitted diseases in this passage about prostitutes. A horde of seemingly new STDs has begun to swarm through America's promiscuous adults and teens, but most of them aren't really new. Some scientists doubt that any of them are really new—they are simply modern manifestations of diseases that have existed as long as sin. We are only seeing mutations that have adapted to overcome our modern antibiotics and serums. The promiscuous are doomed to mourn when their flesh and body is consumed.

The best thing is to do what Joseph did. Run! Flee from youthful lusts. Avoid the pits, the snares, and the deadly traps that satan plants in your path. Choose life and live.

Endnotes

1. Mike Murdock, *Wisdom for Winners* (Tulsa, Oklahoma: Honor Books, 1993), pp. 141-143, 154.

2. Murdock, *Wisdom for Winners*, pp. 141-143, 154.

3. James Strong, *Strong's Exhaustive Concordance of the Bible* (Peabody, Massachusetts: Hendrickson Publishers, n.d.), #H5158 "valley"; #H7796, #H8321 "Sorek."

4. *Strong's*, #H8123 "Samson"; #H1807, #H1809 "Delilah."

Chapter 7

The Deception That Leads to Death

Every *sex trap* devised by satan depends on common elements to make them deadly and efficient. All of them depend on human desire sent in the wrong direction to bring the prey to the trap. But satan's attraction mechanism always includes another crucial element that is designed to bypass our ability to think and analyze, and to neutralize our internal sense of what is right and wrong. I'm talking about *deception.*

Deception takes almost any form conceivable because it is simply the misrepresentation of truth for a devious end. Deception whispers in your ear on a chilly night in the back seat of a car, "If you love me, prove it." Deception justifies the sin you've been tempted to commit with the ancient lie, "Everybody else is doing it." Deception stifles the last protest of your beaten-down conscience with the reassuring words from America's favorite soap opera moralists, "It's all right because we love each other."

In the previous chapter, I mentioned the temptation that I faced after the sudden death of my first husband. I had been married for 24 years when I was turned into a widow in a moment of time. Once I became single, I was dumped unwillingly into the world of the "available widow." I had to adjust to men calling me, grinning at me, and inviting me to go with them to all kinds of places, both inside and outside the country. I had been saved all my life, I was filled with the Holy Ghost at the age of six, and yet I was so naive that I didn't even know which end of a cigarette people are supposed to light (I still don't want to know). I had never experimented with drugs, but I had discovered that I really liked wine more than I should. But then this "holy one of Israel" experienced a new level of reality therapy—when my flesh kicked in.

My restless flesh said, "Girlie girl, now you know that you have prayed for and with some of your peers in the gospel who slipped into a little sin, and...God restored them! They are still preaching, and they still have their anointing. Now you have been good all your life. Don't you think you need a testimony for your ministry? *God will cover you, girl. He is long suffering.* You told folks around the country about God's grace and mercy. You need to find out about that yourself." I was being courted by deception, satan's messenger and emissary.

The devil was lying to me, just as he has whispered lies to you. But I knew that devilish deception only presents one side of the picture. It is designed to entice you, but it will never tell you that it is out to ensnare you. Deception says, "Anything forbidden usually excites." But the reality is that a sex trap, like all traps geared to trap big game, has powerful jaws underneath that irresistible bait. Those spring-loaded jaws are lined with sharp cutting teeth crafted to crush and tear your life to shreds. Instead of the pleasure it promises, the sex trap delivers pain and heartbreak that can affect you and your family for many generations.

Now I need to go into some deep teaching, so take out your pencils, colored pens, and fluorescent highlighters. I want to give you what I call "The Formula of Death." It involves the "Four D's" of destruction that Mike Murdock shared in his book, *Winners.*[1]

Desire
(*your emotions*)

plus

Deception
(*of your intellect*)

leads to

Disobedience
(*by your will*)

which equals

Death

I told you it was deep. "D plus D leads to D which equals D." That's the formula for death. Again, sexual desire is natural and normal. But the direction it takes determines whether you will be blessed or cursed. Satan had dispatched devilish deceivers assigned to compromise believers through deceit for the purpose of killing, stealing, and destroying their spirit, taking away their salvation, stealing their soul, and breaking down the saints' body, soul, and spirit. Satan's allurements may look nice for a short season, but his motives and methods aren't pretty—they are deadly.

So what kind of lies has the devil been whispering in your ears over the past year? Did he use "Deceit Plan #1: Everybody is doing it"? Throw it back in his face and say,

"That's a lie. I'm not doing it. And even if I had done something I shouldn't have last night, you can believe that after today I won't do it tonight! I know God is watching and I want to please Him more than I want to satisfy my craving."

It is a fact that God is watching us at all times. No, I don't think He is up there with a massive baseball bat just waiting to slam us when we do something really bad. I think He watches over us like a shepherd, and if you remember, He is the One who has been known to leave the 99 sheep to seek out the one sheep that was lost and in danger. That is why He often sends someone along with supernatural discernment or gifts to reveal what we try so hard to conceal.

One day I was playing the organ in my church during a Sunday night service, and God's people were offering up praise and worship and just going to town. That was when the Holy Spirit said to my heart, "Look down the aisle." I looked down the aisle and saw a couple walk into the sanctuary. I also saw a bed with blue sheets and a bedspread in the middle of the aisle. I even saw the name of the hotel! I had to look twice just to make sure I wasn't seeing things after a long day. We had three services that day to accommodate the crowds, but I saw the vision again!

I said, "My God, why would You show me something so evil? That's a sweet little girl, and that is a fine young brother. I know them, Lord. They both pay their tithes and they're faithful. They never get in trouble." I could see no way how I, as the wife of the bishop, could tell folks what I had seen. I said, "All right, I'm not even going to tell my husband. This is evil. It's got to be the devil. I'm hallucinating."

I told myself those things again and again, and I was troubled all night long. The next day, my husband went to the hospital to pray for someone and I heard the doorbell ring. The woman whom I had seen in the open vision was standing at my door. I silently asked in prayer, "Lord, does she know what I know?"

"Is the bishop home?" she asked. When I told her that he was out on a hospital call, she said, "Well, the Lord told me to come over here right now, and whoever was here, I was to talk to them. I've got a problem and I have to get rid of it."

I sensed the Lord telling me to take her by her hand and set her down in the kitchen. (Kitchen nooks are wonderful places for "breaking the ice.") The Lord also told me to take the young woman's hand and tell her that I already knew about her problem. When I did, she broke down in tears. I told her the name of the hotel, and I described the blue sheets on the bed and what she and the young man were wearing when they met one another in the hotel room. All she could say was, "Oh my God!"

"Don't be afraid," I said. "That's the love of God for you. Even before you went into that hotel, I want you to know that Jesus had already forgiven you. He made provisions to cover the sin you committed all the way back on Calvary. He doesn't condone what you did or give you permission to do it again, but His Word says that if you will confess your sin, He is faithful and just to forgive you" (1 Jn. 1:9). Then I told her, "I'm not here to judge you. But for the grace of God, I don't know where I would have been found, or what I would have done."

I'm thankful that we serve a God who makes miracles out of mistakes. Yet we need to be aware of five facts about sexual sins that can contribute to satan's deception and lead us to death if we cling to our ignorance. Once again I am indebted to the ministry of Dr. Tony Evans, who shared these "Five Truths About Sexual Sins" and inspired me to include them in this chapter:[2]

1. **To Sin Sexually Is a Choice!** It was Samson's decision to lay his head on Delilah's lap. It was David's decision to continue looking at Bathsheba, to send for her, to commit sin with her. He could have stopped the process at any time, but he chose to act on his desires. Joseph ran from Potiphar's wife and temptation, and it helped him remain victorious. The Old Testament instructs us, "Choose you this day whom ye will serve" (Josh. 24:15). If we choose to serve the Lord, we must deny our flesh its desires, wants, and longings whenever they do not please and bring glory to Jesus.

2. **Anyone Can Commit Immorality.** The Bible says, "All we like sheep have gone astray" (Is. 53:6a). Consider this passage in the Book of Romans: "Thou therefore which teachest another, teachest thou not thyself? thou that preachest a man should not steal, dost thou steal? Thou that sayest a man should not commit adultery, dost thou commit adultery? thou that abhorrest idols, dost thou commit sacrilege?" (Rom. 2:21-22) These verses certainly challenge each of us to know that no one is exempt from the temptation to commit immorality. We must all walk cautiously in the faith by the Word of God. All of us— preachers, teachers, missionaries, evangelists, ushers, hospitality hostesses, armorbearers, choir leaders, singers, musicians—must beware of sex traps that come to destroy us. We can make it victoriously—but only by the grace, mercy, and love of God.

3. **Past Success Is No Guarantee of Future Success!** All too often we underestimate the power of passion. The fact that you haven't fallen into a sex trap

so far today or yesterday has absolutely nothing to do with tomorrow. Many of us testify openly, "I have not fallen into fornication or adultery since I became born again." I caution you to hold that testimony until after you have passed a genuine test with "Brother So-Fine," the wealthy good-looking brother you would be tempted to say "yes" to should he ever ask. If he asked you to "function at the junction" and you said "no," then you can stand up and testify. Yesterday's victory has nothing to do with tomorrow's success.

4. **Immorality Always Brings Consequences.** Although forgiveness is available, it does not "undo" all the consequences of sexual sin! Forgiveness will not restore your torn apart family, the loss of respect, the threat of disease, pregnancy, or the danger that these consequences might quickly escalate to even more serious sin. These need to be considered if you plan to commit sexual immorality. Romans 1:32b says, "They which commit such things are worthy of death, not only do the same, but have pleasure in them that do them."

5. **God Will Forgive You and Set You Free!** God will forgive you. If He forgave David, He will forgive you. You can't change what happened last night or a year ago, but you have a lot to say about what will happen tonight! The Word says, "What shall we say then? Shall we continue in sin, that grace may abound? God forbid..." (Rom. 6:1-2).

Some Christians think that they have a special brand of holiness and superior righteousness because their mama was a missionary or their daddy was a preacher. Some believers hold their noses higher than necessary just because they believe that they live on "the right side of town." The truth is that "sin ain't nothing but sin." Sin comes to the rich and it comes to the poor. It condemns the blacks, the whites, the up, and the down. Our money and skin color have nothing to do with it. If you are living an upright life, I can assure you that it is purely because of the grace and the mercy of the living God that you even have a heart to live right.

When the devil tells you, "Everybody is doing it," you need to tell him, "I am breaking the statistics! I'm starting a new trend. If I was in sin, I won't sin again by the grace of God." Be prepared when the devil shifts gears and says, "Well, you were born like this. You are a born homosexual. You're a born lesbian. You are a born alcoholic—it runs in your family and it always will. You are a born abuser and you come from a long unbroken line of abusers. It's a ghost you'll just have to live with."

Answer the deceiver the same way Jesus answered him. Pull out your sword and whack away at his tongue—the only weapon he has left after his defeat at Calvary. Just tell him:

"Well, I read something different. God says in His Word that I am fearfully and wonderfully made. He says that He created me in His image, and He also mentioned that you are a defeated foe. He told me that if any man be in Christ—that's me—that 'he is a new creature: old things are passed away; behold, all things are become new' (2 Cor. 5:17). I have the spirit of God in me now, and even you know that God is not homosexual. Devil, I think you got confused again. God is not homosexual, so I am not homosexual. Now if that spirit is still hanging around me, I know that the power of the living God can strip and peel if off of me. I am willing to pay the price of my deliverance—'Get thee behind me, satan!' "

If you have repented of your sin and been washed in the cleansing blood of the Lamb of God, then I can guarantee you that the devil hates you now. It has always been the self-appointed task of satan to pervert God's plan and purpose for every person, place, or thing. Satan isn't all-powerful or all-knowing, but he is persistent in his works of evil.

We've already looked at the satanic lie used against leaders like Solomon, the lie that says, "I deserve a reward for all that I have done and endured." Solomon basically said, "I owe it to myself. I have been working for God for a long time. Look at the temples I've built and the wealth that I have brought into the kingdom of Israel. My father brought notoriety, but look what I did...

Thou knowest how that David my father could not build an house unto the name of the Lord his God for the wars which were about him on every side, until the Lord put them under the soles of his feet. But now the Lord my God hath given me rest on every side, so that there is neither adversary nor evil occurrent. And, behold, I purpose to build an house unto the name of the Lord my God, as the Lord spake unto David my father, saying, Thy son, whom I will set upon thy throne in thy room, he shall build an house unto My name" (1 Kings 5:3-5).

Solomon was basically telling the King of Tyre in this passage, "My father David said the temple would be built, but I actually built it. I put Israel on the map. I sacrificed, and worshiped and praised until I nearly dropped. I developed ministries and a kingdom. So I owe myself a good time." Solomon's lofty opinion of himself and his conviction that he "owed himself a good time" dropped him right into the sex trap of polygamy mixed with idolatry. Idolatry is the act of worshiping anything other than God. Solomon felt that since he was the king, the great leader and ruler of Israel, then he had the automatic authority to change any law or rule that prevented him from doing what he wanted to do. He forgot that the greatest laws are handed down to man from God Himself, and that man has no power or right to nullify what God has established.

I run into preachers all the time who have this "The King I Am" attitude. They will proudly tell you, "That's my name on the marquee outside. I have business cards and I do only major meetings—I don't have the time or the interest for smaller meetings." Or they'll say, " 'I' lead praise and worship at conferences. 'I' have developed a ministry of excellence. 'I' have a great vision, and 'I' have great people to execute 'my' great vision."

Solomon's desire to bring pleasure to himself brought about the demise of Israel as a unified nation, removed the throne from his son's control, and resulted in his dismissal from the presence of God. That was real death—separation from the presence of God.

Solomon loved luxury, married pagans, turned to idolatry, and caused Israel to become enslaved. When you are a leader in the Body of Christ and you make wrong choices, you can mess up your whole church. You may even tie up the praises of God in your temple. Your secret unrepented sin can stop the flow of God's anointing to the entire church body.

Remember the secret sin of Achan in the Old Testament. When one man broke the direct command of God and stole something set apart as holy, God's blessing and divine protection suddenly lifted from the entire nation. Men began to die in battles that shouldn't have even been called skirmishes. Israel had to stop and say, "Hey, there is something unholy among us. It is bringing God's wrath into all of our homes. The sin of Achan had put his entire nation in harm's way because God refuses to bless sin or associate Himself with that which is unclean or rebellious." (See Joshua 6–7.)

Our church went through a cleansing one time after God said that something in our "camp" was stinking. Conferences had to be canceled and we went into church-wide times of fasting and prayer. People had to return to the "old ways" and come to the front of the church sanctuary to confess to the brethren, "I have sinned against God and you, my brethren."

When you lie down with men or women all over the city, you aren't just sinning against God. You are sinning against the church body that you represent. You have brought harm to yourself and your brethren, and you need to take responsibility for your sin. You need to go before those whom you have wronged or put at risk and offer them an apology in the spirit of true repentance. Jesus told the chief hypocrites of His day, "Bring forth therefore fruits meet for repentance" (Mt. 3:8). That means you have to give evidence to prove your repentance is more than empty words. It must continue for more than just a week or a year. It needs to be lifelong and heart-deep.

Endnotes

1. Mike Murdock, *Wisdom for Winners* (Tulsa, Oklahoma: Honor Books, 1993), pp. 141-143, 154.

2. Drawn from a chapter in Tony Evans' booklet, *Tony Evans Speaks Out on Sexual Purity* (Chicago: Moody Press, 1995).

Chapter 8

Catch Me, But When You Do...Take Me to Jesus!

God told me a while back that the Church is filled with men and women who are trapped in *sex traps* but who feel helpless to escape. They long to be "caught," because the weight of their sin is unbearable, and they have a faint hope that God might be able to forgive them somehow.

It seems like hardly a week or month goes by that I don't get a phone call, a letter, or a fax transmission from someone who heard me minister this message on "Sex Traps" and has managed to break free by faith in the power of Jesus Christ. Although many of the confessions reveal depravity in "high places," they also display the love and compassion of Jesus Christ. For in spite of depraved leadership, God continuously shows up at meetings and churches throughout the world. He doesn't come because of the leaders, but because He has compassion for the lost, the hurting, and the truly hungry people of God who want out of their sex traps.

I value the lives and confidences shared with me by so many precious men and women in the Body of Christ. Let me just say that *because of the power of God's Word*, many illicit relationships have been discontinued, "shacking couples" have gotten married, pornographic subscriptions have been cancelled; and pastors, teachers, evangelists, and prophets who should have married years ago have been setting wedding dates—all because of God's grace, mercy, and love.

A very special person shared with me the power of God and His forgiveness as she gained the strength and courage to break off a relationship with a married "man of God" who had secretly sustained her emotionally, physically, and financially for several years. She still faces an uphill battle, but she can sleep at night with a clean, clear conscience because she is out of her sex trap! I bless and praise God for this miracle.

Others tell of sexually abusive relationships where they were forced into sexual activity. Although they were paid handsomely for the privilege of abusing their soul and body, the day came when money couldn't cure their pain. Deciding to trust God and His Word, they have given up the fine cars, budget accounts, travel, and living expenses that came with their arrangement of bondage. They gave it all up in exchange for forgiveness and freedom in Christ. They stepped out of their sex traps and have not looked back!

If you are trapped in a sex trap that seems impossibly deep with walls too high to scale, I can tell you right now that God is ready to lift you out of your miry pit. He will snap every yoke of bondage, but you need to repent and turn your life over to Him without reservation or condition first. You may be a victim or a victimizer. You may be the abused or the abuser, the predator or the prey. It doesn't matter. They are all sex traps, and the only one to profit from them is the devil. If you want to be free, then you need to surrender everything—including your addictions, attractions, and cravings—to Jesus Christ.

We were talking earlier in the book about the woman in the Gospels who was caught in the act of adultery. I told you that I was amazed that the religious leaders only brought the woman since it "takes two to tango." I have to tell you that I have my own opinions about that situation, and maybe it has to do with what Jesus wrote in the sand with His finger that day (see Jn. 8:4-11).

Perhaps He wrote, "Where is the man? If you hide him, you share in his sin." No one but God knows what Jesus really wrote, and no one alive on the earth today can tell us who the man in the adultery case was. I submit that he was somewhere putting his three-piece preacher's suit back on and getting ready to preach. He was out there somewhere "getting ready to be deacon on Sunday." He was somewhere other than in the middle of that angry crowd with the woman whom he had be caught with. Perhaps he was getting ready to lead the choir while that poor woman was about to be hung out as a piece of trash. Wherever that man was, he missed out on a glorious deliverance. The woman was caught, but they took her to Jesus...

I have a tip for every young woman reading this book. Get smart. That romantic, hormone-driven, young man of God will strip your clothes off, strip your pride, strip your ministry, take your self-respect, take a shower, put his clothes back on and leave; and you will be left with the accusing fingers pointing at you! He'll be preaching again by Sunday and you will be left with depression, with a disease, or with a baby and no means of support. Get smart and tell them all, even the ones with a seminary or college degree: "No ringey, no dingey."

When that woman was dragged in front of Jesus—probably still in a state of undress and public humiliation—I noticed that no one asked, "Where is the man?" It seems like a logical question to me, and since the Pharisees were always eager to point the finger at anyone outside their number, it is logical to assume, given their peculiar silence this time, that this particular fornicator was a religious fornicator, a "temple pimp" with an eminent academic pedigree. I think that Jesus didn't make an issue of it because He had a greater point to make: He was about to demonstrate in dramatic terms that *sometimes the only way to get out of your sex trap is to get caught.* The woman was caught, and she won her freedom forever. The man's sin was covered and hidden, so he carried it with him the rest of his days unless he repented and came to Christ later on.

When those religious hypocrites caught that woman, they accidentally brought her to the right man. They thought that they would use her to accuse the man from Galilee, but they really brought her to the only One who could cleanse and free her from her captivity. Her accusers thought that they would see her condemned to death by the greatest teacher of the day, but instead they brought her to the only One who could forgive and release her. Evil men brought her to Jesus fully expecting to wound and destroy her by stoning, but they really brought her to the One who alone could make her whole. The accusing scoffers threw her in front of Jesus expecting the crowd to join in the fun and later help end her life, but the Master wrote in the sand and told those *without sin* to cast the first stone. In moments, the two were alone, the accusers run off by their own sin. Jesus stripped her of her shame and restored her life again, but this time He sent her on her way with a simple, all-important message you and I need to remember: "Neither do I condemn thee: go, and sin no more" (Jn. 8:11).

If you are trapped in a trap of satan's devising, then you need to be praying, "Catch me, but when you do, take me to Jesus. Take me to the One who loves me. Take me to the One who died for me. Take me to the One who can make me whole." If you have a friend or neighbor struggling in the depths of sin and despair, look at that person and whisper in his or her ear, "You know, the only way you are going to stop is to get caught."

You can get caught by man, or you can let the Holy Ghost arrest you and catch you today. Now if you let the Holy Ghost catch you, He will cover you and wrap you up and forgive you, and nobody will even know what you are forgiven for. You could be a modern-day "temple prostitute" although no one in your church knows it, and still find forgiveness today. What is a temple prostitute? It is a woman who gives sexual favors and support to men in the Kingdom—without benefit of a marriage certificate.

I notice when I see single men in the church who are always relaxed, comfortable, and worry free. A single man is supposed to be an uncomfortable man. He is supposed to have trouble getting a hot, home-cooked meal. He is not supposed to have sisters in his apartment cleaning up, washing and ironing, taking his clothes to the cleaners, putting gas in his car, and paying the bank notes on his house and car.

"But Sister Wanda, he says that one day, when it is the Lord's time, he is going to marry me." Honey, *he who plays house never gets a house.* You need to tell that "wannabe man" something that even he can understand! Tell him, "If we're not married, then I don't cook for you, I don't wash for you, I don't iron for you, I don't clean for you, I don't baby-sit for you, and I am sure not going to sleep with you!" Tell yourself and anyone else close enough to hear you: "I won't be a temple whore or slut. I choose not to be one. I am special, I am godly, and I am a woman of purpose, promise, and destiny."

Some of the men in the Body of Christ have become "temple pimps," thinking that they need to prove to every woman who comes along that they are a man. They boldly take advantage of women and their money in the Body of Christ. A sexual encounter with a woman will not prove your masculinity, my brother. Neither does a sexual encounter with a wealthy woman afford you finances to fund your visions, plans, and dreams for life. Should a godly man encounter a female sexual aggressor, I would say, "If any woman in the Body of Christ forces, presses, and pushes you to 'see if the sexual shoe fits,' drop her. You are on the brink of falling into a deadly sex trap!" The Bible says in the last days that seven women will grab one man! (See Isaiah 4:1.) They won't even want his money. There are a lot of women who will be happy to satisfy a man's economic dilemma once he agrees to meet their biological and emotional needs...*in a deadly sex trap*!

Are you in a trap today? I believe that all of us have traps in our lives, places where we continually stumble and feel chains of bondage, limitation, and weakness. Too many times we point our fingers and speak harsh words of judgment against brethren or the lost, but the Lord once again tells us what He told the condemning disciples 2,000 years ago:

> *But He turned, and rebuked them, and said, Ye know not what manner of spirit ye are of. For the Son of man is not come to destroy men's lives, but to save them...* (Luke 9:55-56).

Before you judge other people, ask yourself what you would do in their situation. I mentioned earlier in the book that for 20 years and more, I told people, "No ringey, no dingey." Then I became a widow. I began to think about all the other ministers I had known and ministered to because they had failed God and fallen into sexual sins. They repented and were restored, and they are still ministering under the anointing. They still sing and preach the Word of God. When the thought came to me, *Girl, just catch a plane and go to another little country where there are brothers who want to see you. When you come back, nobody will know that you took care of your natural sexual needs.* That was when God said, "I will know. Little girl, don't let those thoughts dwell in your mind too long, for if you even look at someone with lust in your heart, you have committed adultery." I said, "Oh my God."

If it wasn't for the grace of God, this "sister girl" might have never made it down the aisle of matrimony again in the victory of purity—but I did, and all the praise goes to God, and God alone. I can't say that I was "too saved and too holy" to fall—I know I was preserved and held blameless because my God shackled and tied me up in His love, and He patiently reminded me, "Thou shalt not, you will not, you won't!" Let me be real—it sure wasn't because I didn't want to wander to the forbidden side. Whether you want to admit it or not, it is normal to want to. It is natural. It was godly for me to have a desire for a man, but it was not godly for me to share intimacy with any man outside of the marriage covenant. God put the desire in me, and He put it in you. It is the direction that your desire takes that determines if you are going to be blessed or cursed. One of the things the Spirit of God brought to my mind again and again was my position of royalty in His house. He had paid too great a price to redeem and transform me from darkness to light for me to lay it all down just to lie with a man. He made me a queen, and I had no business involving myself in relationships that would diminish who I was in Christ.

Don't Touch Royalty!

More sisters in the Body of Christ need to stand up and tell the men in their lives, "I'm somebody special. You won't take from me what I don't give you. I belong to Another, and if you want something from me, you have to talk to Him and do things His way!"

Many years ago before the "great divorce," Princess Di came from England to the United States for an official visit and the first lady of the United States went to greet the princess upon her arrival. Now it seems to me that the first lady is our equivalent to a queen, am I correct? The first lady stepped out to greet Princess Di like you would expect her to, but when she began to embrace the princess, the security men from England said, "Don't touch royalty." A lot of Americans watching the greeting on television were insulted. "The nerve! That is our first lady—why if she wanted to hit Di, she could do it!" (Of course she never would, and of course Princess Diana was probably as embarrassed by the incident as our first lady.)

The Lord used that incident in the natural realm to teach me something in the spiritual realm. He told me, "You have to understand that you have been washed in the blood of the Lamb of God. Somebody died on the cross for you. You are royal seed because you have been bought with blood. You are special. You are not an average woman, and you aren't a piece of junk. You are of royal blood, and you need to tell the devil whenever he tries to touch you, 'Don't touch royalty!'"

Now I'm telling you: Tell that filthy demon spirit, "Get your lustful hands off of me. I'm royalty!" Many of our problems arise because we don't know who we are in Christ. When you know who you are, you are more careful about the places you go and the people you associate with. When you really know who you are, you carry security with you 24 hours a day.

A good guideline to help guide your decisions and monitor your actions is this: Don't do anything that your security can't watch! Don't lie down with anybody whom Jesus wouldn't want to watch you lie down with (that limits you to your lawfully wedded spouse—*period*). Don't do anything that you don't want your Savior to see.

The time finally came when God led me to Bishop Andrew Turner. After a wonderful courtship, this man asked me to marry him and the time came for me to fly to the East Coast to meet his family. That was how this wonderful *holy woman of Israel*, this woman filled with the Holy Ghost since she was six years old, the wife of the late pastor, the *evangelist of the hour*, found herself in a hotel on a rainy, lonely night. It is dangerous to be in a luxurious hotel suite with a fireplace when it is raining. (I would have had a better time of it if I had been broke and stayed at the Motel Six.)

I watched the rain starting to come down and thought of the wonderful man who had kissed me, hugged me, and told me good-night. The man I ached for had gone back to his family's home and left me all alone in that hotel room. I thought, *I am by myself. That fireplace is going. The music is on* (and it wasn't the Brooklyn Tabernacle, although I love them). Before I knew it, I had that phone to my ear and I called up my Andrew. "Baby, have you made it back home? Well, what are you doing?" He said, "Well, I am just getting ready to go to bed." I said, "You know it is raining, and your little girl is over here all by herself. Ain't nobody with me in this room. I wonder if you could come back over for a few minutes?"

I couldn't believe my own ears. I felt like I was listening to another woman talking on the phone! Sometimes the flesh will surprise you and put you in places and conversations that will amaze you. There "ain't no good thing" in this flesh, and you can't trust yourself. You can only trust the living God. My flesh had me proposition my own fiancé! Yes, this is the Reverend Sister Doctor Wanda admitting to the truth! Praise God for a godly man. Brother Andrew told me, "Wanda, this conversation is not going in a good direction." My flesh wasn't done yet: "But if you love me, you would come back over." (I took a page out of the devil's songbook.)

Andrew said, "Wanda, don't do this. You are pushing me." I kept up the heat and sang another chorus from satan's lullaby: "Baby, if you really cared about me..." Now this was the evangelist, the woman who goes to 5:00 a.m. prayer, and fasts and prays. Now if I faced that kind of challenge and said what I said, what would you do in the same situation without the benefit of prayer and fasting? Don't be deceived: *Sex traps will hit anybody.*

The conclusion to this little sordid story of Wanda's wandering to the dark side is that Andrew stood his ground and Wanda wised up by God's grace. Because Andrew was the man whom God made him to be, and my protector instead of a predator, I was able to walk down that church aisle in total victory, with my self-esteem and honor intact. But if it hadn't been for the grace of God, my foot might have slipped, and my "bumpers and lumpers" too.

I'm sharing this personal story with you because I want you to know that sin has no respect of persons! The devil will use anybody and anything he can to trap you. You have to make up in your mind that you *hate sin*. Admit it and quit it. Make a decision and live it.

One year later as a happily married woman, I heard Andrew talking to his oldest birth daughter about the ways of men and women in the world and in the church. I listened in amazement as he said, "As beautiful as Wanda is to me, if she had laid down with me before marriage, I would not have married her."

You better know that I thank God today that I zipped it up, wrapped it up, tied it up, pulled it up, and told it, "Calm down, girl." My advice to you is serious: *Don't let your desire mess up your miracle.* Don't let your desire steal your blessing and take your promotion.

Chapter 9

Rescue by Repentance, Not Resolution

What do you do when you are in a sex trap? You are hurting, you are bleeding, you are torn, your leg has been bitten, you are spiritually crippled and nearly smothered by the massive weight of guilt and shame. You don't have enough strength to climb out of the pit yourself. Your "paw" was broken by the force of the cruel steel jaws of satan's trap. You don't have any weapon, witty saying, or tool to help you out of it. So what do you do? Do you say, "I'll just die. I deserve it anyway"?

Many of us would either sink deeper into despair over the total disappearance of hope from our horizon, or we would make optimistic resolutions motivated by the emotional trauma of the moment. A large batch of us would try to do both in typical human fashion. The problem is that God isn't calling merely for an apology or even a resolution. He requires something far more costly, yet beneficial in the long run.

God requires repentance, but instead we offer Him something like this: "I am *never* going to do this again. Once is enough for a lifetime. From this day on, Lord, You can count on me. I won't come this way again." This is a sincere and impressive-sounding resolution, but you and I both know that, most of the time, it isn't worth the cost of the paper it's written on. The problem with making a resolution is that it is based on our own strength and determination. Even logic will tell you that if our strength and determination were so great, then how in the world did we end up in a trap in the first place?

We all have to face the truth on this one: We don't have enough strength or virtue for what God is calling for. He demands true repentance that comes from the heart. A man's resolution will never stand up when that sexual desire comes roaring back on the scene. In the face of a genuine *sex trap*, a resolution to "quit" something is as empty as a fantasy that one is trying to overcome.

I would like to say it gently, but it never seems to come out that way. "My friend, if you are in a sex trap, you are going to have to repent." Repentance only comes when your heart has truly changed your outlook on sin. Intellectual assent is worthless when you are in the grip of a satanic trap.

Some of mankind's most brilliant and educated minds have found themselves morally and spiritually bankrupt in the pit of a sex trap—including Solomon. That is why it is a worthless exercise to quit a sex sin by mere resolution. That is like a soldier who is out of ammunition standing up in battle and shouting with all the passion he can muster: "I'm gonna keep on shooting at you until you surrender! My finger's on the trigger—I'm tired of you taking potshots at me. My aim is sure, my determination strong. Take that!" He might as well just point his naked finger at the enemy and shout, "Bang, you're dead," like a little boy playing soldier.

It is the stuff that absurd comedies are made of, but the only one laughing is the devil.

Rescue Comes by Repentance, Not by Resolution

Men and women will only stop their destructive behavior when they have truly repented of their actions in their hearts. As we move closer to the heart of God, we will begin to develop a godly sorrow over our sin. His presence and love have a way of reordering our thinking completely. That is why the prophet Isaiah, who evidently lived an exemplary life, wrote, "Then said I, Woe is me! for I am undone; *because I am a man of unclean lips*, and I dwell in the midst of a people of unclean lips: *for mine eyes have seen the King*, the Lord of hosts" (Is. 6:5).

What does it mean to really repent? It means that you have come to the point where you *admit it and quit it with a sorrowful attitude*. I believe that one reason God makes us cross the threshold of repentance to claim our freedom is that He wants us to imitate the selfless acts of His Son who died on a cross for our freedom.

> *And He [Jesus] said to them all, If any man will come after Me, **let him deny himself, and take up his cross daily, and follow Me.** For whosoever will save his life shall lose it: but whosoever will lose his life for My sake, the same shall save it. For what is a man advantaged, if he gain the whole world, and lose himself, or be cast away? For whosoever shall be ashamed of Me and of My words, of him shall the Son of man be ashamed, when He shall come in His own glory, and in His Father's, and of the holy angels* (Luke 9:23-26).

Most of our sex trap problems would vanish overnight if we would all stop living the lives we want to live and begin living the life God wants to live through us. The Scriptures say,

> *For if ye live after the flesh, ye shall die: but if ye through the Spirit do mortify the deeds of the body, ye shall live. For as many as are led by the Spirit of God, they are the sons of God* (Romans 8:13-14).

I don't know about you, but I've never had the Holy Spirit of God lead me into an adulterous relationship, speaking falsehoods, gossiping, acts of violence, jealousy, hatred, or backbiting sessions at the church social on Saturday afternoon. Anytime I landed where I didn't belong, I knew that I didn't follow the Holy Spirit to that spot—I followed something or someone else, and there wasn't anything "holy" about it.

The apostle Paul told Timothy, "Flee also youthful lusts: but follow righteousness, faith, charity, peace, with them that call on the Lord out of a pure heart" (2 Tim. 2:22). Frankly, a lot of us are a little too old to be trying some of the junk we are doing anyway! Let me talk to the more "seasoned" believer for a moment. You don't even have the energy to do all the stuff you used to do. "I just have to see if I still got it." (You ain't still got it. You left it behind when your birthday cake couldn't handle all the candles anymore.) Sit yourself down before you die before your time. You can swallow two packs of vitamins a day and all the aloe vera juice you want to, but you still won't see 20 again. Set your tired old self down. You should be teaching some young man or woman how to live holy instead of chasing unholiness around and gasping for breath.

The Book of Proverbs tells us, "For the commandment is a lamp; and the law is light; and reproofs of instruction are the way of life" (Prov. 6:23). If you really want some light on the dangers and seriousness of sexual sin, then you need to read the verses that follow verse 23. It won't take long for you to understand why mere resolutions won't even begin to touch the strongholds of your sex trap:

> ...*reproofs of instruction are the way of life. To keep thee from the evil woman, from the flattery of the tongue of a strange woman. Lust not after her beauty in thine heart; neither let her take thee with her eyelids. For by means of a whorish woman a man is brought to a piece of bread: and the adulteress will hunt for the precious life. Can a man take fire in his bosom, and his clothes not be burned? Can one go upon hot coals, and his feet not be burned? So **he that goeth in to his neighbour's wife; whosoever toucheth her shall not be innocent.** Men do not despise a thief, if he steal to satisfy his soul when he is hungry; but if he be found, he shall restore sevenfold; he shall give all the substance of his house. But **whoso committeth adultery with a woman lacketh understanding: he that doeth it destroyeth his own soul.** A wound and dishonour shall he get; and his reproach shall not be wiped away. For **jealousy is the rage of a man: therefore he will not spare in the day of vengeance.** He will not regard any ransom; neither will he rest content, though thou givest many gifts* (Proverbs 6:23-35).

Solomon warns us not to "let her take thee with her eyelids." There are far too many Christian women who are winking and blinking at the brethren in the choir. They are throwing out snares with their eyes, hoping to capture the interest of the ushers, the preacher, or the Sunday school teacher. We need to look those sisters in the face and say, "You aren't going to do that. It is going to stop right now. Focus those eyes on Jesus and let Him transform you, or you are going to wink up something you can't handle. You are going to wink yourself right into a trap!"

We need to constantly check our motives and be quick to repent when we veer off the path into sin. I do a lot of counseling in my pastoral ministry, and when couples come in for professional counseling, I ask both of them, "Do I have permission to ask you anything in front of one another?" Folks who know my style of counseling get nervous when they have something to hide. You can't cure a sin problem until the sin is admitted and folks are ready to quit it.

We have people from every conceivable economic and educational background represented in our inner-city congregation. I've learned in more than a quarter century of pastoring that there are certain telltale signs that show up when there's hanky-panky in the pantry. If I see those symptoms of moral disease, I lose all interest in putting those folks at ease. When they give me permission to ask the questions I need to ask, I sometimes start the session with the million-dollar question: "All right, who is sleeping around? Who is running with a prostitute?"

After they look at each other and pick their teeth up off the floor, I tell them why I hit them between the eyes: "I know you have a good job. You've been paying your tithes and offerings. Now all of a sudden your car has been repossessed, your house note is in arrears, the appliance people came to pick up your refrigerator (even though you only had two more payments on it), your goldfish died, your dog ran off, and the cat is scratching everybody on the block. It's obvious to me that you went broke. I think that's because somebody is running with a whore." Why? Because Proverbs 6:26 declares, "For by means of a whorish woman a man is brought to a piece of bread...."

Fears from the past operate to keep a victim stuck fast in a sex trap. Whether we want to accept it or not, most of us will live most of our lives in the "in between" place. We are doing better than we did before we were saved, but we haven't reached the place in Christ where we know we should be. That is why I love the words of the apostle Paul. He was painfully honest at times, and I respect that. We all need to get to the place where we can say with the apostle Paul:

Brethren, I count not myself to have apprehended: but this one thing I do, forgetting those things which are behind [the past], *and reaching forth unto those things which are before* [God's dream for our tomorrow], *I press toward the mark for the prize of the high calling of God in Christ Jesus. Let us therefore, as many as be perfect, be thus minded: and if in any thing ye be otherwise minded, God shall reveal even this unto you* (Philippians 3:13-15).

It is time for you and I to forget the pain of the past. Our failures are covered by the atoning blood of Jesus Christ. They have no power to hurt us in God's Kingdom—but our minds still carry barbed arrows attached to memories. We need to forget our failures and mistakes of the past and reach forward to our destiny in Jesus. Recognize what God is saying to you: "Behold, I will do a new thing; now it shall spring forth; shall ye not know it? I will even make a way in the wilderness, and rivers in the desert" (Is. 43:19). He means what He says. Do you? If you do, then say, "Yes, Lord. I believe that You are doing a new thing in me. I will yield to Your Spirit and follow You in the way. My strength isn't sufficient, but You are all I need." *That's not a resolution. That is a commitment to a sovereign God.*

Your only path to survival when you are caught in a sex trap is to pray from the heart, "Lord Jesus, I know that if I am going to survive, I only have one hope: that You are sufficient. You alone are my only hope and joy. My life is in Your hands."

Trapped people are desperate people. I am always surprised at the intensity of responses when I obey God and minister this message on sex traps the way He wants me to. Honestly, I fought it for years. I've laid down this message several times, and each time I told the Lord, "It costs me too much. I'm putting my family, my ministry, and my safety on the line every time I go out there and expose the sex traps in the churches." Each time the Lord has come after me and badgered me until I obeyed Him and told the truth about sex traps.

Recently I was asked to minister at a very special conference. The Holy Spirit instructed me to minister on the subject, "Sex Traps," and I admit that I didn't want to do it. I constantly battled thoughts like, "When they hear you on this subject, doors will close and appointments will be canceled." But no matter how much I prayed and studied, the Holy Spirit would direct me back to the message, "Sex Traps."

With much trepidation I stepped to the podium and began to minister to hundreds of people who had gathered in the main auditorium. As I neared the end of my message, the crowd had swelled to thousands. I was about to deliver an altar call when a person suddenly began to scream and came running down the center aisle from the back of the auditorium. (From the attire, I supposed the person was a man.) The Lord spoke through me about the person's cries, *"That is just the sound of deliverance!"*

The Lord seemed to put everyone on hold—including the ushers and security personnel—as the Holy Spirit lifted and turned this person's body around and gently lowered it to the floor. It all happened without a single person laying hands on this individual. There wasn't a single person close enough to touch this person! The miracle of it all was that when the person went down, I thought I was seeing a neatly dressed young man. But when the person arose, I knew without a doubt that we were looking at a transformed *woman*! I was amazed and surprised. She had gone down as a hardened victim of a terrible sex trap, but after God touched her, she somehow became soft, feminine, and beautiful—right in front of our eyes! Then she began to shout with incredible power and joy, "I'm free, I'm free!"

I immediately opened the altars and said, "Those of you who want to get out of your sex trap and be free—come." The people just started to pour down the aisles under the conviction of the Holy Spirit. It was incredible. God Himself had set the stage for a wonderful and unique altar response. He opened the floodgates of mercy and grace and began loosing His people from sex traps right before our eyes!

And so, while others say, "Sister Wanda is just too raw and too natural...that girl needs to tone down," I look back on this experience and on many others and say, "As long as satan is so low-down, conniving, deceitful, and devastating in his attack against men, women, boys, and girls, then I must also remain devastating in my assaults against the kingdom of darkness!" I have received too many letters, phone calls, and audiocassette tapes telling me of the miraculous healings and deliverances that God has worked through the message, "Sex Traps." Even if one person gets delivered through the message of this book, then I can forget and dismiss the complaints of the self-righteous and ultra-religious critics. Yet, I want it publicly known that I desire to offend no one except satan. It is my wish and hope that hurting, helpless, trapped people of God would know that I love them and want them free!

One of the things God told me when He commissioned me to write this book was that people would be delivered right in their homes, offices, apartments, and places of employment if they would agree with the Word of God and the truth of deliverance that this message proclaims. You don't need stained glass windows, pews, or even a church altar to repent. All you need is a repentant heart and a surrendered life—God will meet you where you are and do the rest.

The people who flocked to the altar at the conference I described earlier and at other conferences and services didn't come forward to make "resolutions." Most of them had made enough "resolutions" to fill a small house, and those good intentions hadn't helped them one bit. The only thing they ever got from all their resolutions was more guilt to heap onto what they already had, because none of them could ever keep those resolutions.

No, people run to the altar to repent. They don't run to the front just to enjoy the plush carpet of your church sanctuary, or the nice decor of your community hall. They are rushing to the bloodied cross of Jesus Christ! They are plunging their troubled souls into the Fount of Blood that cleanses away all sin. They have come to the end of all their empty resolutions, and they know that they need to repent of their sin. Once they repent, God can—and will—deliver them and begin His healing work of restoration.

If you are in a sex trap right now, then you can be free today, right now! Forget the resolutions. The first thing you need to do is repent.

Chapter 10

The Four "D's" of Deliverance

Blessed be the Lord, who hath not given us as a prey to their teeth. Our soul is escaped as a bird out of the snare of the fowlers: the snare is broken, and we are escaped. Our help is in the name of the Lord, who made heaven and earth (Psalm 124:6-8).

In almost every area of life, humans seem to have problems with "following through." It can be the kid who has trouble keeping his or her promise to clean the room because a friend shows up with a new bicycle, or the victim of a sex trap who leaves the church building free and delivered—only to head straight for the bait again.

There is a myth in the Church that says once you are saved, you won't ever have any problems, commit any sin, or get mangled by your hang-ups. Yet there are too many people limping around in God's house who are crippled by their recurring sin problems. Their lives are standing denials of the power of God. They are walking billboards that advertise the impotency of their salvation and the worthlessness of their testimony in Christ. Something is wrong in the Church, and I can guarantee you that it has nothing to do with God or the integrity of His Word.

The problem is that we either don't know how to live holy lives, or we are failing to obey God's Word. Most of us have to admit that our problem lies in the second category. Jesus said, "If the Son therefore shall make you free, ye shall be free indeed" (Jn. 8:36). We know that Jesus was speaking truth, so why are so many Christians living a lie?

Multitudes of believers truly have been set free, but they are still hanging around the old broken traps that made them stumble. They keep sniffing at the attractive bait that never seems to leave their minds and emotions. Just as the aroma of food triggers the stomach acids of a hungry man, so the allure of that forbidden bait arouses the foul cravings of our flesh all over again.

Like an accident victim who keeps going back to the scene of a near-fatal crash, we feel the rush of emotions, the crush of our fears, and the hunger of the flesh every time we resurrect the memory of our impact in the trap. Every time we revisit the scene of our sin, we reanimate and revitalize the power of the trap to ensnare our soul again. It is time to stop deceiving yourself: You are about to fall into that sex trap again. Each time you return, it's harder to get back up and out again.

Jesus told the woman caught in the act of adultery, "Sin no more" (Jn. 8:11). He expected her to turn around, to leave her sinful ways behind and never look back. In other words, once Jesus did His part, He expected that woman to do her part. Why would He treat you or me any different? He wouldn't and He isn't. Jesus Christ did His part on Golgotha's tree. My Bible says that just before Jesus died, He cried, "It is finished!" (Jn. 19:30) He meant what He said. Peter elaborated on the details for us:

*According as His divine power **hath given unto us all things that pertain unto life and godliness,** through the* *knowledge of Him that hath called us to glory and virtue: whereby are given unto us exceeding great and precious promises: **that by these ye might be partakers of the divine nature, having escaped the corruption** that is in the world through lust* (2 Peter 1:3-4).

I've made my point. God has provided all the tools, promises, and support we need. We just aren't using them because we aren't obeying His Word. I've said it before, but I need to say it again: When you can't move the enemy, move yourself. Move away from, move out of, move up to, get yourself to a new place where old sins and old traps won't matter anymore. Get to the place where you no longer remember or regard the former things. Make room in your life for God to do a new thing in you. Get away from your problems and plunge yourself—body, soul, and spirit—into His eternal promises.

You aren't a beginner when it comes to sex traps. If you've lived past the age of 13, then you know the familiar pull of hormones, peer approval, and the opposite sex. That means you should be able to spot a sex trap or two when you run into them. Yes, the devil will disguise and hide them, but once you receive Jesus Christ as Lord, He sends the Holy Spirit to stay in your heart day and night. And He told us to follow that Spirit everywhere. He said that the Holy Spirit would guide us into all truth—not every sex trap the rebel devil has laid for us (see Jn. 16:13). It is about time for you to *do what you know to do*! James the apostle put it this way: "Therefore to him that knoweth to do good, and doeth it not, to him it is sin" (Jas. 4:17).

Before I get to the heart of this chapter, let me review a few vital definitions. A trap or snare is "an apparatus contrived and designed to catch, to snare, to hold, to possess, for the supreme purpose to destroy." You won't find very many of satan's sex traps sitting out in the open. Most of them are hidden along familiar trails and paths that you use every day, but the devil is waiting for you to come to the wrong place at the wrong time.

These "familiar paths" are the normal, natural needs and desires God put in us when He created us. They include our need for the following:

1. Love

2. Affirmation

3. Tender intimacy (including sexual intimacy and intimacy outside of sexual relations)

4. Security (physical, mental, spiritual, and financial)

5. Friendship

6. Understanding

7. Nurture

8. Vision and Purpose

9. Guidance and Direction

10. Sexual release

11. Children

12. Goals and Challenges

13. Excitement and Pleasure

14. Personal Fulfillment

Bait is "a carefully prepared deceit, it is death on a stick, an enticement engineered to speak to a corresponding hunger or appetite to lead one from freedom to bondage." It smells good. It looks good. It feels good, and it tastes good—but it is connected to a deadly trap.

Now I want to share with you one of the deepest truths that God has shared with me through a published message by Mike Murdock in his book entitled, *Wisdom for Winners*. It is a deep word for mature believers. It assumes that you have at least a basic knowledge of God's Word, and a personal commitment to do the will of God. If you meet these minimum requirements, then you may be ready to receive the formula that yields life. Are you ready for a deeply spiritual revelation? Are you ready to experience total victory of that sex trap that keeps showing up in your life? Then get out your highligher and colored pencils again. This formula for victory involves four "D" words that I can almost guarantee that you will never forget. Write them down and memorize them:

Don't
Do
Dat
Dummy

Are you impressed? Well, ask yourself, "Do you really want to live?" Then get your behind out of that trap and *don't do dat, dummy*! You won't find a better or simpler formula for deliverance. You need to realize that God is used to working with people who are always falling into the devil's traps. But He isn't interested in making it His full-time work—He already gave us what we need to be free. He is interested in our putting feet to our faith. He wants to see some saints running *away* from temptation instead of *to* it!

But with many of them God was not well pleased: for they were overthrown in the wilderness. Now these things were our examples, to the intent we should not lust after evil things, as they also lusted. Neither be ye idolaters, as were some of them; as it is written, The people sat down to eat

and drink, and rose up to play. Neither let us commit forni-
cation, as some of them committed, and fell in one day three
and twenty thousand. Neither let us tempt Christ, as some
of them also tempted, and were destroyed of serpents. Nei-
ther murmur ye, as some of them also murmured, and were
destroyed of the destroyer. Now all these things happened
unto them for ensamples: and they are written for our ad-
monition, upon whom the ends of the world are come.
Wherefore let him that thinketh he standeth take heed lest
he fall. **There hath no temptation taken you but such as**
is common to man: but God is faithful, who will not suf-
fer you to be tempted above that ye are able; but will
with the temptation also make a way to escape, that ye
may be able to bear it (1 Corinthians 10:5-13).

I challenge you to add something to that Scripture that
isn't already provided by God. You can't because it is all
there. No matter what temptation satan has baited your
hook with, God has made a way of escape!

God wasn't happy with the Israelites in the wilderness
because they kept falling into the same old traps of sexual
sin and idolatry. Every time a believer falls into a sex trap,
by their actions they are putting the attractions of men,
women, experiences, and sexual pleasure before God. This
passage mentions the shocking fact that 23,000 were struck
dead one time for openly committing fornication in front of
God's face. What would happen if God came to Toledo, Los
Angeles, Dallas, or New York City and killed everyone who
had committed adultery? I am afraid that in these days, you
wouldn't have many folks left—*even in the churches.*

The Scriptures say, "Neither let us tempt Christ, as some
of them also tempted, and were destroyed of serpents"
(1 Cor. 10:9). Some of us keep telling everyone in the church

on testimony night, "Oh, that devil's been after me again," but the truth is that God is bringing judgment to our house because we're not taking care of business. We keep returning to our favorite sin and trying to cover it by saying, "The devil made me do it." He didn't have to. You walked over to the edge of the pit and hopped in!

Don't
Do
Dat
Dummy

If you really want to be free from your sex trap today, God can deliver you. He can set you free in the blink of an eye, but you will have to take some personal responsibility to *stay free!* If drinking is your problem, then stay away from bars. If Mary Sweethips on Fifth Avenue is your problem, then keep your lips away from Ms. Sweethips. *Don't do dat, Dummy!* If so-called "recreational drugs" are your problem, then stay away from every place and every face that reminds you of your "high." Stay away from the boys in the 'hood. Stay away from the places you should. Do the good you know to do, and don't do the bad you know you shouldn't do.

Take responsibility for your actions. Discipline your conduct. Discipline your prayer life. Discipline yourself in what you see and hear. Become involved in your local church worship. Actively invest in your freedom. Lift your hands to God and say,

Father God, in the name of Jesus I give You permission to break those sex ties off of me. I give You permission to break every soul tie that binds me to the past and to the things You have forbidden.

Sever me from my history. Change my resumé. Rewrite my biography. Free me. Flip me. Get me out of that trap. I will

stand still and let You fill me while the Holy Ghost does His work in me.

I will let the precious blood of Jesus and the living Word wash over my mind, cleanse my emotions, purify my spirit, and sanctify and anoint my body for Your work.

Lord Jesus, take control of my memory. Push the "reject" button. Push the control button that gets rid of evil and harmful things. Push the command button that wipes out that painful memory of my failures, mistakes, and past weaknesses. Take the bitter taste of sin and shame out of my mouth.

Renew a right spirit within me. Take the bitter taste of rejection and lack out of my emotions. Set me free. I won't move until You tell me to move. I open my mouth and invite You to fill it with Your words of life, Lord.

I believe every word You have spoken is true, Lord God. I thank You for setting me free and doing the work of a Redeemer in my life. I thank You because Your Word has set me free. I thank You because You are changing me! You are pulling me right out of my trap. You are releasing me from the pain and setting me free from my anguish. You are delivering me from every bit of bitterness. I give myself to You, body, soul, and spirit. In Jesus' name I pray and will stay, Amen!

It feels good to be free at last, doesn't it? I have a final word for you from the Lord Jesus Christ:

> **My child, where are your accusers?**
> **Can anyone condemn you now that you are washed in My blood?**
> ***Then go, and sin no more.***

ther *exciting titles*
by Dr. Wanda Davis-Turner

I STOOD IN THE FLAMES

If you have ever come to a point of depression, fear, or defeat, then you need this book! With honesty, truth, and clarity, Dr. Davis-Turner shares her hard-won principles for victory in the midst of the fire. You can turn satan's attack into a platform of strength and laughter!

Paperback Book, 154p. ISBN 1-56043-275-6 Retail $7.99

Don't miss any one of these exciting videos by Dr. Wanda Davis-Turner. These messages can change your life!

SEX TRAPS
1 video   ISBN 0-7684-0030-9   Retail $14.99

PRIVATE DELIVERANCE IN A PUBLIC PLACE
1 video   ISBN 0-7684-0054-6   Retail $14.99

REMEMBER TO FORGET
1 video   ISBN 0-7684-0048-1   Retail $14.99

THE OTHER MIRACLE
1 video   ISBN 0-7684-0053-8   Retail $14.99

GOD'S ORIGINAL PLAN FOR THE FAMILY
1 video   ISBN 0-7684-0049-X   Retail $14.99

Available at your local Christian bookstore.

Internet: http://www.reapernet.com

Prices subject to change without notice.

Other
Destiny Image titles
you will enjoy reading